265
Troubleshooting
Strategies for
WRITING
NONFICTION

Barbara Fine Clouse

McGraw·Hill

New York   Chicago   San Francisco   Lisbon   London   Madrid   Mexico City
Milan   New Delhi   San Juan   Seoul   Singapore   Sydney   Toronto

Library of Congress Cataloging-in-Publication Data

Clouse, Barbara Fine.
  265 troubleshooting strategies for writing nonfiction / Barbara Fine Clouse.
    p.   cm.
  ISBN 0-07-144539-0
  1. English language—Rhetoric—Handbooks, manuals, etc.   2. English
language—Grammar—Handbooks, manuals, etc.   3. Report writing—Handbooks,
manuals, etc.   I. Title: Two hundred and sixty-five troubleshooting strategies for
writing nonfiction.   II. Title.

PE1408.C535   2005
808'.042—dc22   2004026245

1 2 3 4 5 6 7 8 9 0   FGR/FGR   0 9 8 7 6 5

ISBN 0-07-144539-0

McGraw-Hill books are available at special quantity discounts to use as premiums and
sales promotions, or for use in corporate training programs. For more information, please
write to the Director of Special Sales, Professional Publishing, McGraw-Hill, Two Penn
Plaza, New York, NY 10121-2298. Or contact your local bookstore.

This book is printed on acid-free paper.

For Jeff, Greg, and Karen Clouse, with love

Contents

Acknowledgments

I am grateful to Lisa Moore, Anne Stameshkin, Ruth Smith, Michele Pezzuti, and Ellen Vinz of McGraw-Hill for their support and expert guidance. In addition, I owe much to the sound counsel of the following reviewers, whose insights inform this book:

Steven E. Cohen, Norwalk Community College

Lahcen Elyazghi Ezzaher, University of Northern Colorado

Donald Erskine, Clark College

Carol S. Manning, Mary Washington College

Sue McIntyre, Humboldt State University

Robbi Nester, Irvine Valley College

Deborah Coxwell Teague, Florida State University

Julie Whitlow, Salem State College

Finally, to my understanding husband, Denny, and to my children, Greg and Jeff, I offer thanks for the support and for the room of my own.

Introduction

*Myths About Writing: Don't Believe
Everything You Hear*

People say many things about writing. Some of what they say is true, and some is not. Let's see if you can tell the difference between the facts and the myths.

Which of the following statements are facts, and which are myths? (The answers appear after the list, but don't peek.)

- Writers are born, not made.

- "Good" writers write fast.

- Writers should wait for inspiration.

- "Good" writers rarely struggle.

- "Good" writers get it right the first time.

- Outlining is very time-consuming.

- The longer the words, the better they are.

- Revising is reading over a draft and fixing spelling and punctuation.

- After drafting, "good" writers look for their grammar mistakes right away.

- There is only one way to write.

- A well-stated point does not require proof.

- After making their last point, writers should just stop.

- Sentence fragments are always short.

- Run-ons and comma splices are always long.

- Use a comma wherever you pause in speech.

- Capitalize a word to emphasize it.

- There are no rules to explain English spelling.

- The longer the writing, the better it is.

Much of what you hear about writing just isn't true, including the preceding statements: every one of those statements is a common myth about writing.

How to Become a Better Writer

Myth: Writers are born, not made.

"I'm a terrible writer." People say this all the time, and maybe you have said it yourself. If so, you are probably wrong. More likely, you are not as good a writer as you could be—or would like to be—but now you have the chance to become a better writer, even an excellent one.

Maybe you think you can't be a good writer because you weren't *born* a good writer. Again, you are mistaken, for you can *learn* to be a good writer. Becoming a better writer has much in common with becoming a better swimmer, piano player, or dancer. In all these cases, you can work to improve a skill. As you work to improve your writing skills, think about the following habits of highly successful writers:

Habits of Highly Successful Writers

1. **Be patient.** Improving a skill takes time. Just as perfecting a foul shot takes a basketball player time and practice, so too does improving your writing. If you expect too much too soon, you will become frustrated. Expect to make slow, steady progress rather than dramatic, overnight improvement.

2. **Expect to get stuck.** Everyone does, even experienced professional writers. Writer's block and dead ends are all part of writing, so do not think something is wrong with you if you have some trouble. Consult this text, and talk to experienced writers when you get stuck. When you solve the problem, tuck the solution away for future reference, so the same problem does not plague you over and over again.

3. **Remember that writing is really *rewriting*.** Experienced writers work and rework drafts several times. With each revision, know that you are acting like an experienced writer.

4. **Talk to other writers.** Find out what they do when they write, and try some of their procedures. Form a network with other writers for support and suggestions.

5. **Study the responses to your writing.** Share your writing—either in draft or finished form—with people with good judgment. Ask them what they think and why. Reader response is valuable to a writer. By paying attention to this response and working to improve areas where readers see weaknesses, you can improve more quickly.

6. **Read, read, read.** Read every day—the newspaper, newsmagazines, short stories, romance novels, crime novels—anything that interests you. Notice how other writers do things. Pay attention to how they handle beginnings, endings, proof of their ideas, sentence structures, punctuation, and transitions. Try to incorporate some of their techniques in your own writing. The more you read, the more you learn about the nature of language and the faster your writing will improve. Furthermore, frequent reading makes you more knowledgeable, so you have more ideas for your writing.

7. **Do not fear mistakes.** They are a natural part of learning. Take risks; try things out. If you make mistakes, embrace them as opportunities to learn. If you are afraid of making a mistake, you will never try; if you never try, you will never grow. Try to connect your mistakes to your writing procedures. Decide which procedures work well for you and which do not. Then consult this text for procedures to replace the ones that did not work. For example, maybe drafting goes well for you, but revising does not. That means you need to discover new revision procedures. You can read about those procedures in this book and then try them out. When your procedures work better, your writing will improve.

Understand That Writing Is a Process

Myth: "Good" writers write fast.

Very few worthwhile endeavors are accomplished quickly, and writing is no exception. Successful writers typically engage in a number of activities, and doing so takes time. These activities include the following:

1. Prewriting (coming up with ideas and finding a good order for them)

2. Drafting (writing up your ideas in a preliminary form)

3. Revising (improving the content and expression of ideas in your draft)

4. Editing (finding and correcting grammar and usage mistakes)

Writers do not always move in a straight line from prewriting to drafting to revising to editing. Instead, they often double back before going forward. While drafting, for example, you may think of a new idea to add. By doing so, you have left drafting and doubled back to prewriting. Or while editing, you may think of a better way to phrase an idea. Then you have left editing and doubled back to revising. Never consider any stage of the process "done" and behind you. Always stand ready to return to an earlier stage when a good idea strikes you.

Now let's consider what each stage of writing involves.

Prewriting

Myth: Writers should wait for inspiration.

If you sit around waiting for inspiration, you may never get anything written; inspiration does not occur often enough for writers to depend on it. In fact, inspiration occurs so rarely that writers must develop other ways to get ideas. Collectively, the procedures for coming up with ideas in the absence of inspiration are called **prewriting**. The term *prewriting* is used because these procedures come before writing the first draft.

Chapters 1 to 3 describe procedures for coming up with ideas to write about and for discovering ways to order those ideas.

Drafting

Myth: "Good" writers get it right the first time.

Once writers generate enough ideas during prewriting to serve as a departure point, they make their first attempt at getting those ideas down. This part of the writing process is **drafting**. Typically, the first draft is very rough, which is why it so often is called the **rough draft**. The rough draft provides raw material that can be shaped and refined in the next stages of the writing process. Chapters 4 to 8 describe drafting procedures.

Revising

Myth: Revising is reading over a draft and fixing spelling and punctuation.

During **revising**, writers rework the raw material of the draft to get it in shape. This reworking is a time-consuming, difficult part of the process. It requires the writer to refine the content so that it is clear, points are adequately supported, and ideas are expressed in the best way and best order possible. Chapters 9 to 16 describe revising procedures.

Editing

Myth: After drafting, "good" writers look for their grammar mistakes right away.

Because experienced readers expect your writing to be free of errors, you must **edit** to find and eliminate mistakes so they do not distract or annoy your reader. Many writers hunt for errors too soon, however, before they have revised for content and effective expression. Editing should really be saved for the end of the process.

Chapters 17 to 27 describe editing procedures.

Develop Your Own Writing Process

Myth: There is only one way to write.

Although this book often mentions *the* writing process, there really is no single correct process. Instead, writers develop procedures that work well for them; so every successful writer can have a different, successful process. As you use this book and work to become a better writer, try different procedures for prewriting, drafting, revising, and editing. Some of these procedures will work well for you, and some will not. Continue sampling until you have effective strategies for handling all the stages of writing, and at that point, you will have discovered your own successful process.

PART 1

A Troubleshooting Guide to Prewriting

Has this happened to you? You write some sentences, but when you read the material over, you hate it. You wad up the paper or hit the delete key, and then you begin again. But the same process repeats itself over and over. This is writer's block. Or perhaps you never get anything on paper or on the computer screen. Instead, you just stare at the blank page or screen, trying to squeeze out ideas. This, too, is writer's block. Fortunately, you can banish writer's block with the strategies described in this section on prewriting. (**Prewriting** refers to the ways writers discover ideas to write about.)

"I don't know what to write."

The terror of the blank page! No, it's not a movie coming soon to a theater near you. It's the fear writers experience when they sit down to write but cannot think of anything to say. Sure, sometimes writers are zapped by the lightning bolt of inspiration, and idea after idea comes tumbling forth. Inspiration is fickle, however, and cannot be counted on to just show up. Therefore, if inspiration fails you, take steps to develop ideas on your own. The following strategies, known as **idea-generation techniques**, can help you come up with ideas when inspiration does not arrive on time.

Troubleshooting Strategies

1 ← *Freewrite*

The act of writing stimulates thought, so when you cannot think of anything to write, start writing anyway. Eventually, ideas will surface. With **freewriting**, you write to discover ideas to write about. It works like this: Sit in a quiet spot and write nonstop for about ten minutes. Record every idea that occurs to you, no matter how silly or irrelevant it seems. Do not stop for any reason. If you run out of ideas, write the days of the week, names of your family members, even "I don't know what to write." Write *anything*. Soon new thoughts will strike you, and you can write about them. The important thing about freewriting is to be *free*, so make wild statements, write silly notions, or make random associations. Do not evaluate anything; if it occurs to you, write it down. Do not worry about grammar, spelling, punctuation, or neatness—just write ideas the best way you can without worrying about anything. Here is a freewriting sample produced to discover ideas for writing about the effects of computers:

Computers are wonderful and scary at the same time. They are great because they make things easier and faster, like writing things and getting info. Let's see, what else? They store info and trade it with other computers so our privacy can be invaded, that's pretty scary. Laptop computers are big now, you see people use them everywhere. That's good and bad because you can work when it's convenient but you also work when you should be resting. This whole Internet thing is weird. People spend whole days on it. Is that productive or lost time? What else? Pornography is a problem on the Internet and kids can get involved. Yuck. Now what else? I'm stuck, I'm stuck. If you don't understand computers, you will have trouble in the job market. I guess that means schools better do a good job of teaching this stuff. Now what? Anything else? Expensive. Who can afford all this computer equipment? Is it just for the rich? I read an article that said computers are changing the way we communicate. I don't remember what all it said, I should look it up.

Notice that the freewriting unearthed a number of ideas for writing about the effects of computers: convenience, possible invasion of privacy, changes in the way people work, the time spent on the Internet, changes in the way people communicate, the need for schools to educate children in computer skills, and whether or not computer access is just for the rich.

2 ← *Use Looping*

With **looping**, you explore a topic in more depth by freewriting a second and sometimes a third time. For example, the previous freewriting sample on the effects of computers yielded several ideas for writing, including "the time spent on the Internet." To use looping, you would freewrite on this topic for ten minutes. That second "loop" may yield enough material, or you may freewrite a third loop on an idea that emerged in the second loop. Taken together, all the freewriting loops can bring forth considerable material.

3 ← *Try Clustering*

Clustering lets you see at a glance how ideas relate to one another. To cluster, write in the middle of a page a subject area you want to think about. Then draw a circle around the subject, so you have something that looks like this:

Next, as you think of ideas, connect them to the central circle:

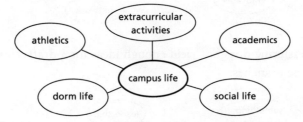

As more ideas occur to you, connect them to the appropriate circles:

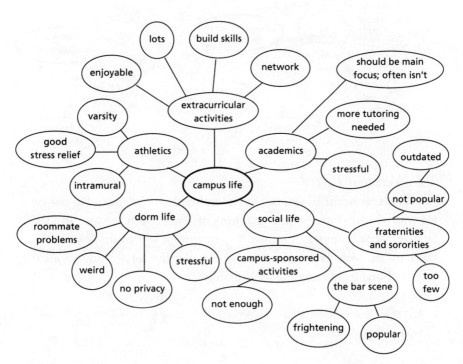

Continue writing ideas and joining them to circles until you can think of nothing else. Then study your clustering to see if one particular circle with its connecting circles gives you enough ideas to begin a draft. For example, this portion of the previous clustering might serve as a departure point for a draft about the benefits of extracurricular activities:

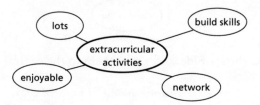

If this clustering does not yield enough ideas for a draft, cluster again to expand the branches:

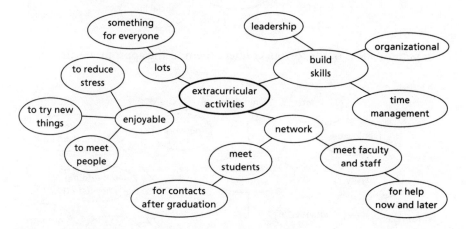

4 ← *Write a List*

List ideas that occur to you in phrases rather than sentences. Do not censor yourself; write everything you think of. Even if you are sure an idea is terrible, write it anyway, because it may prompt you to think of another more useful idea. Here is an idea-generation list for writing about the effects of being cut from the basketball team:

felt rejected
was embarrassed

disappointed my father
got teased
felt inadequate
gave up basketball forever
decided to go out for cross-country
lost my best friend, who was busy with the team

Next, review your list and cross out ideas you do not want to use and add new ideas that occur to you. If you number the ideas in the list in the order you want to treat them in your draft, you have a scratch outline. Sometimes you may want to write a second list focusing on only one of the points in your first list. For example, a second list focusing on "lost my best friend, who was busy with the team" could look like this:

Cal had no time for me
practiced every day
couldn't go out at night because of curfew
socialized with his teammates
wouldn't play sports with me because of fear of injuries

5 ✦ *Brainstorm*

To **brainstorm** for ideas, ask yourself questions about your topic. The answers can provide details for your essay. Sometimes the question that offers up the most information is the simple question "Why?" In addition, you may find the following questions helpful:

Why did it happen?
How did it happen?
Who was involved?
When did it happen?
Where did it happen?
Could it happen again?
What does it mean?
How does it work?
Why does this matter to me?

Why does this matter to my reader?
Why is it true?
What is it similar to?
What is it different from?
What are its physical characteristics?
Why is it important?
Who would care about it?
What causes it?
What are its effects?
What is it related to?
What examples are there?
How can it be explained?
What controversies are associated with it?

6 ← *Examine Your Topic from Different Angles*

If you have a broad subject area you want to write about, but you are not sure how to limit the subject, try viewing it from different angles. Asking yourself the following questions can show you how to approach your topic from different perspectives:

1. **How can I describe my subject?** What does it look, smell, taste, sound, and feel like? What are its parts, color, size, shape, and so on?

2. **How can I compare and contrast my subject?** What is it like, and what is it different from? Are the similarities and differences important?

3. **What do I associate my subject with?** What does it make people think of? What is it related to? What does it develop from or lead to?

4. **How can I analyze my subject?** How is it broken down? How does it work? What is it made of? Why is it important?

5. **How can I apply my subject?** What is it good for? Who would find it useful? When is it useful? Does it have social, economic, or political value?

6. **What arguments accompany my subject?** What are the reasons for it? What are the reasons against it? Who is for it? Who is against it? Is it right or wrong? Good or bad? How does it affect society?

After answering these questions, you may have an approach to your subject.

Then you can do some additional idea generation for ideas to suit your approach.

7 ← Use Questionnaires

Learning what other people think can expose you to fresh perspectives and stimulate your own thinking. To discover what others think, develop a questionnaire for people to complete. This is not a scientific instrument; it is just something to prime your own idea pump. For example, say you want to write about the movie rating system. You could develop the following questionnaire:

1. What do you think of the current movie rating system, which uses the designations G, PG, PG-13, R, and X?

2. Why do you think the way you do?

3. What could be done to improve the system?

4. What aspects of the current system should remain the same? Why?

Your questionnaire should not include too many questions, or people will not bother with it. Nor should you use the answers *instead* of your own thinking; the answers are meant to stimulate your own thinking. Finally, question at least five people so you get a useful number of responses.

8 ← Write an Exploratory Draft

When you do not know what to write, sometimes the solution is to get in there and write anyway. You may be one of those people who don't know what they want to say until they say it. If so, sit down and force yourself to write on your topic for about an hour without worrying about how good the material is. The result will be an exploratory draft—a few pages of material reflecting what you currently know.

An exploratory draft may yield a thought or two that you can pursue with one of the idea-generation techniques in this chapter, or it may yield enough for you to try an outline or rough draft. Remember that your goal is not to produce a first draft; it is to discover one or more ideas to serve as a departure point.

9 ← *Relate the Topic to Your Own Experience*

Relate the topic to your own experiences so you can write about what you know. For example, to write about modern technology, remember all the trouble your cell phone caused you, and write about how this device can be more trouble than it is worth. To write about the American educational system, think about your child-care hassles and argue that your company should have a day-care center. A topic that seems formidable at first can be made manageable if it is viewed in the context of your own life experiences.

10 ← *Talk into a Tape Recorder*

Forget writing for a while and try talking. Have a conversation with yourself about your topic by speaking all your thoughts into a tape recorder. Do not censor yourself; just talk about whatever occurs to you, and feel free to be silly, offbeat, funny, dramatic, or outlandish. When you run out of ideas, play back the tape. When you hear a good idea, pause the tape and write the idea down.

11 ← *Talk to Other People*

Discuss your writing topic with friends and relatives. They may be able to suggest ideas. Or have other people ask you the brainstorming questions that appear earlier in this chapter.

12 ← *Write a Poem*

Sometimes changing formats can help, so instead of trying to write an essay, write a poem about your topic. Then study it for ideas you can shape and develop in prose form.

13 ← *Write About Your Block*

When all else fails, write about why you can't write. Explain how you feel, what is keeping you from getting ideas, and what you would write if you could. This sheer act of writing can catapult you beyond the block to productive idea generation.

14 ← *Put Your Writing on the Back Burner*

If you do not know what to write, you may need to give your ideas an incubation period. Try going about your normal routine with your writing topic on the back burner. Think about your topic from time to time throughout the day. Many writers get their best ideas while walking the dog, washing the car, sitting in a traffic jam, or cleaning the house. If you feel anxious, exercise to relieve the tension. Of course, if an idea strikes while you are in the middle of something, stop and write the idea down so you do not forget it.

15 ← *Identify Your Purpose and Audience*

You may have trouble thinking of ideas if you have not clarified your purpose and audience. Responding to the following questions can help.

To Identify Your Purpose

- What feelings, ideas, or experiences can I relate to my reader?

- Of what can I inform my reader?

- Of what can I persuade my reader?

- In what way can I entertain my reader?

To Identify Your Audience

- Who could learn something from my writing?

- Who would enjoy reading about my topic?

- Who could be influenced to think or act a certain way?

- Who is interested in my topic or would find it important?

- Who needs to hear what I have to say?

16 ↫ *Keep a Journal*

Buy a full-size spiral notebook for keeping a journal, or set up a computer file. Write in your journal every day. A journal is not a diary, because it is not a record of your daily activities. Instead, it is an account of your thoughts and reactions to events. For example, if you feel compassion for a blind person you saw, describe your feelings. If you are anxious about an upcoming event, explain why you are concerned. If you were recently reminded of a childhood event, describe this memory. A journal is also a good place to think things through in writing. Is something troubling you? Do you have a problem? Explore the issues in your journal, and you may achieve new insights. In addition, if you are working on a writing project, a journal is an ideal place to try out an approach to part of the draft, or to tinker with a revision.

Because your journal is meant for you and not for a reader, you do not need to revise and edit anything. Just write your ideas down in any way that suits you, because you are your primary audience this time. Later, if you are looking for a writing topic, review your journal for ideas. Set aside at least fifteen minutes every day to write in your journal. If you have trouble thinking of what to write, try one of the following suggestions:

1. Write about something that angers you, pleases you, or frustrates you.

2. Describe the ideal education.

3. Write about some change you would like to make in yourself.

4. Look at a newspaper and respond to a headline.

5. Write about someone you admire.

6. Describe your life as you would like it to be in five years.

7. Tell about one thing the world could do without.

8. Record a vivid childhood memory.

9. Describe your current writing process, including what you do to generate ideas, draft, revise, and edit.

10. Describe one piece of legislation you wish you could draft. Explain how it would improve the world.

17 ← *Combine Techniques*

Combine techniques any way you like. Perhaps you will begin with freewriting and then brainstorm. Or maybe you will talk into a tape recorder and then list. Experiment until you find the combination of techniques that works the best.

18 ← *Use a Computer for Idea Generation*

If you use a computer, you may like the following strategies.

Freewrite. With a blank screen, write whatever comes to mind about your subject (or even your lack of a subject). Do not go back with the delete, backspace, or left arrow key. Just write for about ten minutes. Then get a printout, and read what you have typed. Underline usable ideas. Perhaps there will be enough to get you started. If not, do a second freewriting, focusing on the underlined ideas. (For more on freewriting, see the beginning of this chapter.)

Write Blindfolded. No, you don't really blindfold yourself or even close your eyes. Just find the switch that controls the brightness of the monitor and turn it all the way down until the screen is dark. Then type for ten minutes, just as you would if you were freewriting. When you are done, your screen may look like this:

I kdont know what to write I think I;ll write about the problems of students are getting wripped off on the fees and tuition being changerd.

This is not a problem. You can still detect the seeds of good ideas to expand on in a draft or in a second blindfolded writing.

Write E-Mail. Write an e-mail to a friend, and discuss your writing topic. Mention the ideas you currently have, and ask for a response to those ideas and for some additional ideas to consider.

List and Write a Scratch Outline. You may appreciate listing on the computer because ideas can be easily reorganized and deleted to get a neat, sequenced list of ideas. Just write the first idea that comes to mind. A word or a phrase will do just fine. Press the enter or return key. Write another idea, and press the enter or return key. Repeat these steps until you run out of ideas. Use your delete key to eliminate ideas you want to strike from your list. Next, study your list and decide what order is suggested. Try out the order using the copy-and-paste sequence. Rearrange your list as often as you like until you have a suitable scratch outline to guide your first draft.

Use the Internet. The Internet can be a helpful resource for writers who need ideas. In particular, you might try the following:

• **Surf the Internet.** Type a subject into a search engine, and scan the titles returned for possible writing topics or ideas for developing a topic. Four popular search engines are
AltaVista: altavista.com
Google: google.com
Yahoo: yahoo.com
All the Web: alltheweb.com

• **Browse news sites.** Scan one of these popular news sites for information on current events, health, business, and entertainment. You might get several writing ideas.
Yahoo News: http://news.yahoo.com/?u
Reuters News Service: reuters.com/news.jhtml
Google News: news.google.com

• **Browse electronic newspapers and magazines.** Try one of these sites:

For newspapers around the country and world: refdesk.com/paper.html
An online magazine: http://slate.msn.com
A national newspaper: usatoday.com

• **Browse websites with links to varied content.** These two sites, in particular, may give you writing ideas:

SciTechDaily Review: scitechdaily.com
Arts & Letters Daily: aldaily.com

"How do I determine my thesis?"

You might know in your own mind what your writing is about, but that is not enough. You need to convey that idea to your reader in a clear, appealing way—and that's where your thesis comes in. Your **thesis** is the statement of your writing's focus, and it frequently appears at or near the beginning of your writing.

Because your thesis guides the course of your writing, it must be crafted with care. The suggestions in this chapter can help.

Troubleshooting Strategies

19 ← Study Your Idea-Generation Material

You may be tempted to base your thesis on the point you generated the most ideas for, but that point may not be your best choice. Perhaps you have too much material for the length you are working with, or perhaps that point holds little interest for your reader. Study your idea-generation material carefully with your reader in mind before deciding on your thesis idea.

20 ← Write a Two-Part Thesis

One part of your thesis should give the topic you are discussing, and the other part should note your assertion about that topic. In the following examples, the topic is underlined once, and the assertion is underlined twice:

> <u>The television ratings system</u> <u>does not serve the purpose it was intended to serve</u>.
> <u>The federal government</u> <u>should outlaw Internet gambling</u>.
> Although <u>textbooks</u> cost a great deal of money, they <u>are one of the best bargains in education</u>.

21 ❧ Note the Main Points That Will Be Made in Your Essay

In addition to noting your topic and your assertion about that topic, your thesis can indicate the main points you will cover in your writing (although it does not have to do this). In the following example, the designated main points are underlined:

> Year-round schools are a good idea because <u>children would not forget material over long summer breaks</u>, <u>child care would not be a problem for working parents</u>, and <u>a greater number of elective courses could be offered</u>.

22 ❧ Limit Your Topic to Something Manageable

Avoid treating more than one topic or more than one assertion. Also avoid single topics that are too broad. Treating more than one topic, more than one assertion, or a very broad topic requires you to write too much, or it forces you into a very general, superficial treatment of your topic.

More than one topic:	To revitalize the city, tax incentives should be offered to new businesses, and more parking should be offered downtown.
Better (one topic):	To revitalize the city, tax incentives should be offered to new businesses.

Better (one topic):	To revitalize the city, more parking should be offered downtown.
More than one assertion:	Voters would be less apathetic if campaign finance laws were changed, and if candidates debated more often.
Better (one assertion):	Voters would be less apathetic if campaign finance laws were changed.
Better (one assertion):	Voters would be less apathetic if candidates debated more often.
Too broad:	The American political system needs to be overhauled.
Better:	The electoral college is no longer a sensible way to elect a president.

23 ← *Express Your Assertion in Specific Words*

Words like *good, nice, awesome, bad,* and *interesting* are too vague to give your reader a clear indication of your assertion. So opt instead for more specific words and phrases.

Vague: Jennifer Juarez makes a <u>good</u> candidate for City Council.
Better: Jennifer Juarez is a qualified candidate for City Council because of her extensive political background.

Vague: New York's Metropolitan Museum of Art is an <u>awesome</u> place.
Better: Because of the number and variety of its holdings, New York's Metropolitan Museum of Art is a national treasure.

24 ← *Avoid Factual Statements*

If your thesis is a statement of indisputable fact, your essay will have nowhere to go.

> **Factual statement:** The zoning board must decide whether to approve a housing development on Route 193.
>
> **Better:** The zoning board should approve the housing development on Route 193.

25 ← *Consider Your Thesis to Be Tentative*

During drafting and revising, everything is part of a discovery process and, therefore, subject to change. Your thesis, no matter how carefully you crafted it, is tentative. It may change later, as new insights occur to you.

26 ← *Use a Computer to Help Determine Your Thesis*

If you compose at the computer, try the following strategies.

E-Mail a Friend. If you have trouble composing a thesis, e-mail your idea-generation material to a friend. Ask that person to review the material and to identify one or more thesis statements that seem to emerge from that material.

Use the Internet. For additional information on how to write a thesis, visit these websites:

• Capital Community College's Guide to Grammar and Writing: ccc.commnet.edu/grammar. Select "Index" in the drop-down box under "Essay & Research Paper Level," then click on "Thesis Statement."
• Purdue University's Online Writing Lab: http://owl.english.purdue.edu. In the search box, type "thesis."

"How do I get my ideas to fit together?"

OK, so you've come up with good ideas and now you need to get your ideas to hang together in a coherent whole. The strategies in this chapter can help.

Troubleshooting Strategies

27 ← *Check Your Thesis*

Your thesis tells what your writing is about. (For more on the thesis, see Chapter 2.) If your ideas do not come together, the problem may be with your thesis. Check your thesis against the guidelines that follow, and make any necessary revisions.

• **Be sure you have a thesis.** Can you point to or write out a specific sentence or two that expresses the focus of your writing? If not, your ideas may be nothing more than a collection of loosely related thoughts, which seem confused because they do not develop one central focus.

• **Be sure your thesis expresses an idea worthy of discussion**, something that is disputed or something in need of explanation. For more on this point, see Chapter 2.

• **Be sure your thesis does not take in too much territory**, or you will be forced to bring in too many ideas, which can create disorder.

Thesis covering too much territory: High school was a traumatic experience.

Acceptable thesis: My first high school track meet was a traumatic experience.

The first thesis requires the writer to cover events spanning four years—which could be a great deal for one writing. The second thesis sets up a more reasonable goal: the events of one afternoon.

28 ← *Write a Scratch Outline*

To write a scratch outline, list all your most important points. Then review the list and number the points in the order you will handle them in your writing. A scratch outline can be made quickly, and many writers find it useful. However, because the outline is not very detailed (it covers only the main points), other writers find it does not provide enough structure. If you are one of the latter, you may prefer one of the other outlining techniques described in this chapter.

29 ← *Construct an Outline Tree*

The outline tree provides a visual representation of how ideas relate to each other. To construct a tree, write your thesis on the page:

A refundable deposit should be added to the price of products in glass containers.

Next, branch your main ideas off from your thesis idea:

A refundable deposit should be added to the price of products in glass containers.

to reduce litter   because voluntary recycling is not working   to keep prices down

Then, branch supporting ideas off from your main ideas:

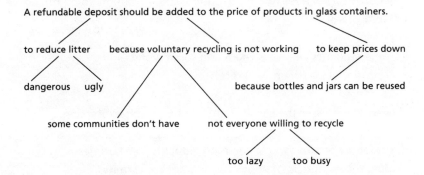

The outline tree shows you how ideas relate to each other so that when drafting, you avoid skipping randomly from one idea to another.

30 ← *Write an Informal Outline*

Writers who are uncomfortable with the formal outline that uses Roman numerals, capital and lowercase letters, and numbers often like the informal outline that lists and groups the most important ideas. Typically, an informal outline includes:

- The thesis idea

- The major points to support the thesis

- Some of the ideas that support the major points

Here is an example of an informal outline for the following thesis: "Public school students should not have to wear uniforms."

Introduction or Opening Paragraph
Mention the problems public schools face (attendance, violence, low-test scores, and demoralized teachers and students), and explain that uniforms are not the solution to these problems.

Paragraphs to Support Thesis
The Constitution does not allow public school students to be forced to wear uniforms.

- Some students will wear them and some won't.
- Preferential treatment will result.

If everyone dresses the same, there will be no self-expression.

- Students need to express their individuality in a harmless way.
- Most other aspects of education require conformity.

Deal with the argument that uniforms save money and eliminate "clothing competition."

- The savings isn't worth the problems uniforms cause.
- People need to learn how to handle competition.

Closing
The problems in our schools must be solved somehow, but uniforms won't do it.

31 ← *Construct an Outline Map*

To develop the map, use your list of generated ideas to fill in a copy of the form shown in Figure 1.

To complete the map, write in your thesis and place one main point at the top of each column. (If you have two main points, you will have two columns; three main points will mean three columns; and so on.) In the columns under each main point, write the supporting ideas that will develop the main point. Then note what your concluding point(s) will be.

You can write your draft from the map by allowing each column to be a paragraph.

Figure 1 Outline Map

Thesis: _____

Main Point	Main Point	Main Point	Main Point
Supporting Detail	Supporting Detail	Supporting Detail	Supporting Detail

Concluding Points: _____
_____
_____
_____
_____

32 ↞ *Write an Abstract*

An **abstract** is a very brief summary. Before you start drafting, write a one-paragraph abstract of what you plan to say in your writing. Include only the main points, and leave out the details that will expand on those points. Then read over your abstract to check that the main points logically follow one to the next. If they do not, try another abstract, placing your ideas in a different order. When you draft, you can flesh out the abstract into a full-length piece of writing.

33 ← *Use a Computer to Help Organize Your Ideas*

Computers can be very handy for helping writers organize their ideas.

The Scratch Outline. If you use a computer to generate ideas by listing, you can turn your list into a scratch outline very easily. Use the delete key to eliminate the ideas that you do not want to use (and if new ideas occur to you, add them to the list). Then by using the copy-and-paste command, arrange the ideas in the order you want to treat them in your writing.

The Outline Program. If your computer has an outline program, use it to fill in the various levels designated by Roman numerals, letters, and numbers. Study the results, and expand and delete sublevels as necessary.

Create Your Own Outline File. If your word-processing program does not include an outline feature, develop your own outline form, using Roman numerals, letters, and numbers. Save the form as a file you can retrieve whenever you want to make an outline. You can also create forms and files for the outline map and outline worksheet.

Use the Internet. If you want to learn the mechanics of writing a formal outline, visit Purdue University's Online Writing Lab at http://owl .english.purdue.edu/handouts/general/gl_outlin.html.

PART 2

A Troubleshooting Guide to Drafting

Drafting is your first attempt to write your ideas on the page or computer screen. Because it is your *first* effort, your draft will probably have many problems. That's normal. In fact, most people write very rough first drafts and then rework them until they are polished and reader-ready. In other words, do not feel discouraged if your drafting yields a very ragged piece of writing. Rough though it is, that draft is useful raw material that you can refine.

"I know what I want to say, but I can't say it."

So you think you know what you want to say, and you sit down with plenty of fresh writing paper, pencils sharpened to a lethal point, and a bowl of Doritos. Then disaster strikes: you know what you want to say, but the words don't come out right—or they don't come out at all.

If this happens to you, know that you are not alone. Plenty of writers experience the same block. To get past the block, use the techniques described in this chapter.

Troubleshooting Strategies

34 ← *Get Rid of Distractions*

Are you trying to write with headphones on? With the TV on in the background? With your roommate rummaging for a missing left sneaker? With the street department outside tearing up the pavement with an air hammer? Few people can write when distractions disrupt their focus, so getting past writer's block may be as simple as finding a place to write that is free of distractions.

35 ← *Set Intermediate Goals for Yourself*

At the beginning of a writing project, the finish line can seem so far away that we feel stress. This stress can lead to writer's block. Try breaking the task down into manageable steps. For example, the first time you sit down, tell yourself you will just come up with five ideas and a scratch outline. The second time, you will just draft the opening. The third time, you will draft two paragraphs. If you work toward the completion of intermediate goals, the project will be less intimidating.

36 ✦ *Allow Your Draft to Be Rough*

If you find yourself starting a draft, crumpling up the paper and pitching it to the floor, starting another draft, crumpling up the paper and pitching it to the floor, starting another draft, and so forth, you may be expecting too much too soon. Remember, a first draft is *supposed* to be rough. Instead of wadding up that draft, force yourself to go from start to finish in one sitting to get raw material that you can shape during the revision process later.

37 ✦ *Write in a New Place*

A change of scene can help a writer break through a block, so if you usually write in one place, try another. Go to the library, the park, or a local diner. If you write in your bedroom, try the kitchen or a coffee shop. A new locale can give you a fresh perspective.

38 ✦ *Switch Your Writing Tools*

If you write with a pen, try a pencil or a computer. If you use a computer, try a pen. If you like lined paper, try unlined. If you like legal pads, try stationery. Do anything to make the writing *feel* different.

39 ✦ *Write on a Daily Schedule*

Professional writers are disciplined about their work. They make themselves sit down at the same time each day to write for a specific number of hours. Follow the lead of the professionals, and push past the block by forcing yourself to write at a certain time each day for a specific length of time.

40 ← *Write a Letter to a Friend*

Sometimes we think of the reader at the other end judging our work, and we freeze. Try writing your draft as if it were a letter to a friend—a letter to someone who cares about you and who will value you regardless of how well you write. When your audience is shifted to a person you feel comfortable with, you can relax and allow the words to emerge. After writing a draft this way, you can revise to make your work suitable for your intended reader and to shape it into an essay or other appropriate form.

41 ← *Write for Yourself Instead of for a Reader*

Forget your reader for a while, and write the draft in a way that pleases *you*. Be your own audience at first. Later when you polish your work, you can make the changes necessary for the audience you are aiming for.

42 ← *Use a Natural Style*

Sometimes writers try so hard to achieve what they think is a "sophisticated" style that the strain causes a block. To solve this problem, write as you normally speak, and the words should flow more easily. After drafting this way, revise if the writing is too conversational or informal.

> **Unnatural:** The garrulous male juvenile, who upon cursory examination gave the appearance of being about twelve, nettled the orator.
>
> **More natural:** The talkative boy, who looked about twelve, annoyed the speaker.

43 ← *Speak into a Recorder*

Sometimes we have trouble writing but no trouble talking. Try speaking your draft into a recorder. Afterward, you can transcribe the recording to get your draft.

44 ← *Reread Often*

If you get blocked in the middle, go back and reread your draft from the beginning. Doing so can give you momentum and propel you past the block. Rereading can be a reminder of your thesis, purpose, and organizational strategy, a reminder that keeps you on track.

45 ← *Walk Away*

When the words won't come, you may need time away to relax and let things simmer. Take a walk, listen to music, play tennis, take a shower, make a sandwich, read a magazine, clean a drawer, or pot a plant. Do anything to clear your mind for a while. Time away can provide an incubation period, so when you start to write again you are no longer stuck.

46 ← *Write the Beginning Last*

If you're stuck on the opening, write the middle and end, and then go back to your beginning. With the rest of your draft complete, you may find your opening easier to handle than it was before. (If you write your opening last, write a thesis on scratch paper so you have a focus for your draft.)

47 ← *Begin in the Middle*

Begin writing about whatever point you feel confident writing, and go from there. Starting with an idea you can write—no matter where in the draft it falls—can propel you forward.

48 ← *Concentrate on What You Can Do, and Skip What You Can't Do*

You can start out just fine, but then begin to struggle along the way and eventually come to a full stop. Why does a good start fizzle? This may happen because you dwell on the trouble spots and lose momentum. To solve this problem, skip the trouble spots: if you cannot think of the right word, leave a blank and add it later; if you sense some detail is not working, underline it for later consideration and press on; or if the right approach to your opening escapes you, begin with your second paragraph and go on from there. You will make more progress by focusing on what you *can* do and leaving the problems behind to deal with later.

49 ✦ *Resist the Temptation to Rewrite as You Draft*

If you constantly rewrite what you have already written, you can get stuck in one place—maybe polishing the introduction over and over, or perhaps tinkering endlessly with the detail to support your first point. While some writers do well if they revise as they go, others get bogged down. If you get bogged down, try pushing forward even if what you have already written is in pretty sorry shape. You can revise the rough spots later.

50 ✦ *Write Fast, and Don't Look Back*

If you write fast, you will have no time to worry about how well you are saying things. You will only be able to get things down the best way you can at the moment. Later when you revise, you can rework things as needed.

51 ✦ *Write an Outline*

If you have generated a number of good ideas and you still have trouble writing a draft, you may be unsure what idea you should write first, second, third, and so on. An outline can help. (For information on outlining, consult Chapter 3.)

52 ✦ *Return to Idea Generation*

You may *not* have a clear enough idea of what you want to say, so you may need to return to idea generation. Try a favorite technique to clarify your thinking or to flesh out some existing ideas. Or try a technique you have not used before (see Chapter 1 for suggestions).

53 ← *Use a Computer to Help You Find the Right Words*

If you like to compose at the computer, the next techniques can be helpful.

Split Your Screen. On one part of the screen, display your outline or idea-generation material; on the other side, display your draft. This way, you can easily refer to your prewriting material as you write. You can also place your thesis in one of the screens to help you stay on track as you draft.

Write Invisible Notes. Many word-processing programs allow you to write notes that appear on your screen but not on the printed page. If you want to remember a question, record an idea, or make a comment for later consideration, and you do not want to interrupt your drafting, use this capability to write on your draft. The comments will not appear on your paper copy, but they will be saved in the computer file for you to come back to.

Cut and Paste. If you generate ideas on the computer, you can cut and paste some or all of that material into a first draft. Of course, you will need to revise that material later, but it can work well as a departure point.

Use the Internet. The following Web page has information on what causes writer's block and how to prevent and deal with it: suite101 .com/welcome.cfm/writers_block.

"I'm having trouble with my opening."

The first day of school, the first day on a new job, a first date—starting out something new can be hard. Starting out a piece of writing can also be difficult, even if you have generated plenty of ideas. The strategies in this chapter can help.

Troubleshooting Strategies

54 ← *Explain Why Your Topic Is Important*

Why should anyone take time to read what you write? Let your readers know why your topic is important, and you can engage their interest. Say your work will explain to the residents of your town how they can eliminate cigarette advertising on billboards. Your introduction can explain why residents should want to eliminate this advertising in the first place:

Other than the tobacco companies and a few nicotine addicts who live in denial, few people dispute the fact that cigarettes are a serious—even a deadly—health hazard. Because cigarettes are so dangerous, laws prohibit their advertising on television. Unfortunately, a similar ban does not exist for print media. As a result, many people are enticed to begin smoking after viewing the ads that promise everything from "pure smoking pleasure" to fun, friends, and romance. Teenagers and younger children are particularly vulnerable to the seductive advertising, and we must protect them. While we cannot force national advertisers to stop running magazine advertisements, we can lobby local officials to ban cigarette advertising on billboards in our town.

55 ← *Provide Background Information*

What should your reader know to appreciate or understand your topic? What information would establish a context for your essay? The answers to these questions can provide background information in the introduction. For example, assume you will argue that more federal money should be spent to educate children about the dangers of tobacco. Your introduction could supply background information about past efforts in this area:

In the late 1990s, President Clinton began an initiative to reduce tobacco use by children. The public was invited to comment, public officials made grand speeches, the press covered the proceedings extensively, and the result was a few Food and Drug Administration efforts to reduce access and limit the appeal of tobacco products for children. Basically, all that this amounted to was some billboards and public service announcements on television. The effects have been minimal, and the public health crisis is worsening as children start smoking at younger ages. Clearly, the federal government must devote considerably more money and resources to educating children about tobacco.

56 ← *Tell a Story*

Create interest in your topic by telling a story that is related to that topic or in some way illustrates your thesis. For example, if your essay shows that modern conveniences can be more trouble than they are worth, the following introduction with a story could be effective:

The morning of my job interview, I woke up an hour earlier than usual and took special pains with my hair and makeup. I ate a light, sensible breakfast, which managed to hit bottom despite the menagerie of winged insects fluttering around my stomach. I drove the parkway downtown, nervously biting my lower lip the whole way. I had to park three long blocks from the office building where the interview was to take place, and by the time I got to the building I was completely windblown. Breathless, I gasped my name to the receptionist, who explained that my interview would have to be postponed. The personnel director had never made it in. It seems her electricity was off, and she could not get her car out of the garage, because the door was controlled by an electric opener. That's when I knew for sure that modern conveniences can be downright inconvenient.

57 ← Use an Interesting Quotation

If someone has said something applicable to your thesis and said it particularly well, you can engage interest by quoting the remark. Just be sure that the quotation is interesting and not an overused expression like "better safe than sorry" or "the early bird gets the worm."

Everyone seems to agree that we learn from our mistakes and that failure can be more instructive than success. As General Colin Powell has said, "There are no secrets to success. It is the result of preparation, hard work, learning from failure." Why, then, are students denied the opportunity to repeat courses without penalty? So we can profit from our mistakes, the administration should allow us to take courses three times and record the highest grade on our transcripts.

58 ← Provide Relevant Statistics

Relevant statistics, particularly if they are surprising, can engage a reader. Just be sure that you note the source of the statistics you use, so your reader does not think you pulled them from the air.

According to our campus newspaper, this college has spent $25 million for campus renovations in the last five years. During the same period, enrollment has dropped by 2,273 students, and 112 fewer people are employed here. These figures suggest that the administration cares more about buildings than people. It is time to reverse the trend and work to increase enrollment, faculty, and staff.

59 ← *Find Some Common Ground with Your Reader*

Identify a point of view or experience you and your reader share. Presenting this common ground in an introduction can create a bond between reader and writer.

In the following introduction, the common ground is a shared school experience:

Think back to when you were in high school. Remember the kids who caused all the trouble, the ones who disrupted the teacher and made it difficult for the rest of the class to learn? They were the students who did not want to be in school anyway and made things miserable for the students who did want to be there. Now imagine how much more learning would have occurred if the troublemakers had been allowed to quit school and get jobs. If we abolish compulsory attendance, everyone will be better off.

60 ← *Describe Something*

Description adds interest and liveliness to writing.

At five feet three inches and 170 pounds, Mr. Daria looked like a meatball. His stringy, black hair, always in need of a cut, kept sliding into his eyes, and his too-tight shirts would not stay tucked into his too-tight polyester pants. He wore the same sport coat everyday; it was easily identified by the grease splotch on the left lapel. Yes, Mr. Daria was considered a nerd by most of the student body, but to me he was the best history teacher on the planet.

61 ← *Begin with the Thesis and the Points You Will Discuss*

Sometimes the direct approach is the best. You can begin by stating your thesis and the main points you will discuss, like this:

Carolyn Hotimsky is the best candidate for mayor for two reasons. First, as president of city council, she demonstrated leadership ability. Second, as chief investment counselor for First City Bank, she learned about sound fiscal management.

62 ↤ *Keep It Short*

If you are having trouble with something, it makes no sense to make it as long as possible. Thus, if your opening is proving troublesome, just write your thesis along with one or two other sentences, and get on with the rest of your writing. If all else fails, just write your thesis and go on to your first point to be developed.

63 ↤ *Write It Last*

If you cannot come up with a suitable opening, go on to write the rest of your piece and then return to the beginning. With the rest of your writing drafted, you may find that an approach to your opening comes to mind. If you skip your opening, however, jot down a working thesis on scratch paper and check it periodically to be sure you do not stray into unrelated areas.

64 ↤ *Use a Computer to Help with Your Opening*

If you use a computer, you may like the following techniques.

Windowing. If you cannot decide which of two or more approaches to use, execute the command that lets you divide your screen in half. Then try one approach to your introduction in one half of the screen and another approach in the other half. Compare the two approaches, and decide which works better.

Turn Your Ending into a Beginning. Your last paragraph may work better as an opening than as a closing. To find out, execute the command that allows you to move your last paragraph to the beginning of your writing. With some fine-tuning, you may be able to turn that ending into a strong opening. Of course, you will have to write a new closing, but that may prove easier than wrestling with the beginning.

Use the Internet. These Web pages offer helpful information on writing introductions:

• The Nuts and Bolts of College Writing has examples of strong and weak introductions at http://nutsandbolts.washcoll.edu/beginning.html #opening.

• George Mason University's online writing center offers a guide to introductions and conclusions at gmu.edu/departments/writingcenter /handouts/introcon.html.

"How do I back up what I say?"

You may be a warm, wonderful human being and as honest as they come, but no experienced reader will believe you unless you support your statements with proof and explanations. The suggestions in this chapter can help you back up what you say.

Troubleshooting Strategies

65 ✦ *Use Your Own Experience*
Your own life experiences can provide convincing evidence. Say, for example, that you are discussing problems created by computers, and you make the point that computers often contribute to procrastination. You might write a paragraph like the following, based on your own experience:

Computers can be great time wasters. The last time I sat down to write a column for our local theater group's newsletter, I found myself playing solitaire instead of drafting. The next thing I knew, an hour had gone by. I got myself back on task, but when I became stuck, I decided to check my e-mail. By the time I read and responded to five messages, another 20 minutes was lost. I tried to work again, but I was lured away by my favorite chat room. I couldn't believe it when the clock in the corner of my screen showed that I had spent an hour discussing the new Alanis Morissette CD. When I realized how much time I had wasted, I went straight back to writing, but I was so tired that I know I didn't give it my best efforts. I probably would have done better had I used a pen and paper.

66 ← *Use What You Observe*

Your observations of the world can offer excellent support for ideas. Say you are discussing the trend to require volunteerism in high schools. Your observation of the volunteer work students do at local high schools could lead to this paragraph:

Students can learn a great deal when they are required to perform volunteer service. However, care must be taken with the kinds of activities they are allowed to engage in. At our local high school, students were at first involved in such worthy activities as volunteering in hospitals, purchasing groceries for elderly neighbors, and coaching youth soccer. Now they receive volunteer credit for such dubious activities as helping out in the school office during study hall, working on theater sets for the senior play, and selling programs at football games. I doubt very much is learned from such work.

67 ← *Tell a Story*

Search your own experience for brief stories that can drive home your points. Consider this passage:

Distance running is an excellent sport for adolescents because even if they do not finish near the front of the pack, they can still feel good about themselves. Shaving a few seconds off an earlier time or completing a difficult course can be a genuine source of pride for a young runner.

Now notice how the addition of a brief story helps prove the point:

Distance running is an excellent sport for adolescents because even if they do not finish near the front of the pack, they can still feel good about themselves. Shaving a few seconds off an earlier time or completing a difficult course can be a genuine source of pride for a young runner. I remember a race I ran when I was sixteen. I was recovering from a miserable cold and was not in peak condition. Just after completing the first mile, I developed a cramp in my side. However, I was determined to finish, no matter how long it took me. Quarter mile by quarter mile, I ran rather haltingly. My chest was tight from lack of training because I had been sick, and my side hurt, but still I kept on.

Eventually, I crossed the finish line, well back in the standings. However, I could not have been more proud of myself if I had won. I showed that I had what it took to finish, even though the going was tough.

68 ← *Describe People and Places*

Description creates vivid images that help the reader to see and hear the way you see and hear. It also adds interest and vitality to writing. Consider this passage:

The best teacher I ever had was Mrs. Suarez, who taught me algebra in the ninth grade. But even more than teaching me algebra, Mrs. Suarez showed me compassion during a very difficult time in my life. I will always be grateful for her understanding and encouragement when I needed them most.

In the ninth grade, I was a troubled teen, a victim of a difficult home life. Somehow Mrs. Suarez recognized my pain and approached me one day. . . .

Now notice the interest created with the addition of description:

The best teacher I ever had was Mrs. Suarez, who taught me algebra in the ninth grade. But even more than teaching me algebra, Mrs. Suarez showed me compassion during a very difficult time in my life. To look at this woman, a person would never guess what a caring nature she had. With wire-stiff hair teased and lacquered into a bouffant, Mrs. Suarez looked like a hard woman. Her face, heavily wrinkled, had a scary, witchlike quality that befitted the shrill voice she used to reprimand fourteen-year-old sinners who neglected their homework. She always stood ramrod straight with her 120 pounds evenly distributed over her orthopedic shoes.

Many a freshman has been frightened by a first look at this no-nonsense woman. However, appearances are, indeed, deceptive, for Mrs. Suarez was not the witch she looked to be. In fact, I will always be grateful for her understanding and encouragement when I needed them most.

69 ✦ *Give Examples*

Nothing clarifies or proves a point like a well-chosen example. Examples can come from personal experience, observation, reading, research, or classroom experience. Assume you have stated that television commercials cause us to buy products we do not need. You could back up that point with examples you have observed, like this:

Television commercials often make people want products they do not need. For example, Tony the Tiger urges children to eat highly sugared cereal, while gorgeous, bikini-clad women romp on the beach, luring men to consume beer. Before Christmas, expensive toys based on the latest action hero are advertised relentlessly, until children are convinced they cannot survive without them. Of course, the worst offenders are the advertisers of hair dye, mascara, lipstick, perfume, and teeth-whiteners, who convince women they cannot be attractive without a drawer full of these products.

You could also take an example from personal experience (the time you went to a tax preparer because a television commercial wrongly convinced you that you could not do your own taxes); you could draw an example from research (talk to others about unnecessary products they have purchased as a result of commercials); or you could cite an example you learned reading a magazine (perhaps statistics on the number of people who have bought a particular unnecessary product).

70 ✦ *Give Reasons*

Reasons help prove that something is true. Let's say your point is that standardized testing should be eliminated. These reasons could help prove your point:

Standardized tests create too much anxiety; they do not really show what a student knows; placing considerable emphasis on one examination is not fair; some students test poorly.

Here is how those reasons might appear in a paragraph:

Standardized tests should be eliminated because they are not a sound educational practice. For one thing, these exams create too much anxiety among students. They worry so much about their performance that they lose sleep, stop eating, and show other signs of stress. Certainly, they cannot demonstrate what they know under such circumstances. They also cannot show what they really know, because the tests cannot test all of a body of knowledge—but just what the state wants to test. As a result, some of what a student knows may never be asked for. Furthermore, if the test is poorly constructed (and many of them are), students may further be kept from demonstrating their real learning. Then there is the fact that many students are poor test takers. They may know the material just fine but be incapable of demonstrating their knowledge because they have never mastered the art of test taking.

71 ✦ Show Similarities or Differences

Assume you are writing about ways to improve the quality of life in nursing homes, and you make the point that nursing homes should allow residents to have pets. The following paragraph shows how you can back up your point by citing similarities:

Because nursing homes have long recognized the value of having young children visit residents, preschool classes are often invited to spend time in the facilities. Allowing the residents to have pets would be similarly beneficial. Just as the children do, the pets would provide companionship for the residents and give them an opportunity to express affection. Also, just as interaction with children does, the interaction with pets would provide intellectual stimulation and an opportunity to forget about infirmities. Of course, in one respect, pets are better than children: they do not have to go home at the end of the day, because they already are home and can continue to make life better for residents.

Now assume that you want to argue that having pets in nursing homes is *not* a good idea. Showing differences can help you back up your point:

Some people claim that having pets in nursing homes would be beneficial in the same way that having preschoolers there is beneficial. This is not true.

First, children will not add cost to a nursing home or its residents. Their parents feed them and take care of medical expenses, but the residents or nursing home would have to assume these expenses for pets. Also, because children are supervised by their teachers while in the facility, residents need not watch them very closely. Pets, on the other hand, need to be restrained from entering the rooms of residents who do not want to be near them. Since many residents cannot supervise the animals all the time, an already overburdened staff would have even more responsibility. Finally, children go home at the end of the day, but pets stay and require ongoing care, which can drain nursing home resources.

72 ← Explain Causes or Effects

If you are writing about sex education in schools and make the point that it should be mandatory, you can back up this point by citing the positive effects of sex education, like this:

Sex education's most obvious benefit is increased knowledge. Since it is unlikely that sexually active teens will start to abstain, increased knowledge about birth control will prevent unwanted pregnancy. Furthermore, the same knowledge can help teens protect themselves against sexually transmitted disease. When fewer teens become pregnant, more of them will stay in school and thus will not fall victim to unemployment, drugs, and crime. When more teens protect themselves against sexually transmitted diseases, fewer will die.

If you want to emphasize the need for sex education by citing the pressure on teenagers to become sexually active, you might explain what causes teenagers to become sexually active, like this:

One reason teenagers are sexually active at a younger age is that they are bombarded by sexual messages. On MTV, videos are populated with women wearing next to nothing; men and women are touching, groping, and grinding in sexually provocative ways. On the radio, rock lyrics glorify teen sex as healthy rebellion and a sign of independence. Movies, too, send sexual messages. Sex scenes and nudity are frequent in PG-13 movies and are standard fare in R-rated movies, which teens get into with no trouble at all.

To discover causes, ask yourself, "Why does this happen?" The answers may provide your details. Similarly, to discover effects, ask yourself, "After this happens, then what?" The answers may provide details as well. For example, ask, "Why do teenagers engage in sex?" and you might get the answer, "To be more like an adult." The desire to be mature then becomes a cause. Ask yourself, "After sex education courses are offered, then what?" If you get the answer, "Teenagers learn safe sex practices," you have an effect of sex education.

73 ✦ *Explain How Something Is Made or Done*

Assume you are discussing simple things people can do to combat prejudice. If you make the point that people do not have to put up with racial, ethnic, or sexist humor, you might back up that point by explaining how a person can deal with such humor, like this:

Many people do not know how to respond when they are told a racial, ethnic, or sexist joke, so they smile or laugh politely, even though they feel uncomfortable. A better approach is to say something simple, such as, "I don't find such jokes funny." Then, you can quickly turn the conversation to some neutral topic. If the joke was told to several people, and you do not want to embarrass the speaker, draw him or her aside later and say, "I'm sure you did not mean to, but you made me very uncomfortable when you told your joke." Both of these approaches let the speaker know that hurtful jokes are not universally welcome.

74 ✦ *Explain What Would Happen If Your View Were Not Adopted*

Say, for example, that you are arguing for the passage of a tax levy to fund the building of a new high school. To help make your point, you can explain what would happen if the levy did *not* pass, like this:

Without the passage of the levy, funds would not be available to finance a new high school. Yet without the high school, our children will suffer. The current building is too small, and enrollment is projected to increase over the next five years. Thus, classes will be seriously overcrowded. Furthermore, the current building lacks an auditorium, making it impossible to have a theater program. The lack of an auditorium also means assemblies and band concerts must be held in the gym, where the acoustics are poor and the seats are uncomfortable. Most worrisome is the fact that the renovations required in the existing building, including asbestos removal, a new roof, and updated heating system, will cost almost as much as building a new school. If we spend money on these renovations, the children will reap no benefits, certainly not the way they would with a new building.

75 ← Consider Opposing Views

Think about the view of those who disagree with you. You can acknowledge a compelling point and offer your counterargument. For example, if you were arguing in favor of warning labels on CDs with sexually explicit lyrics, you could write the following:

People against warning labels cite the "forbidden fruit" argument. They say that young people will be encouraged to buy music with the labels, expressly because they are being warned away from them. To some extent this is true. However, the labels will still provide a guideline for parents who want to buy music for their children. They will also create an atmosphere of acceptability. Although young people may ignore them, the labels still send a message that some things are more appropriate than others for teenagers. This atmosphere is an improvement over the current "anything goes" climate that sends the message that teens can buy and do whatever they please. Down the road, stores may even refuse to sell labeled music to those under twenty-one.

76 ← Use Material from Outside Sources

Statistics, facts, quotations, and ideas from outside sources can provide important support for many topics. These sources can include newspapers, magazines, and sources you discover in the library or on the Internet.

77 ↤ *Use a Computer to Help You Support Your Topic*
If you use a computer, these strategies can help back up your ideas.

Use the Word Count Feature. Sometimes, the number of words that develop an idea can be a clue to how well developed the idea is. Most word-processing programs will tally the number of words you have written. If you are using Microsoft Word, highlight the section discussing the idea in question. Then go to "Tools" in the menu bar and then "Word Count." You will be given the number of words in the document or in a section you highlight. Although the word count is not by itself a reliable indication of sufficient support, it does offer one measure for you to consider.

E-Mail a Reliable Reader for Ideas. If a passage of your draft needs more backup, try e-mailing that section to a reliable reader and asking for suggestions.

Use the Internet. You can use the Internet for research to find quotations, statistics, facts, and informed opinions to help back up your points.

   • Type your topic into your favorite search engine to locate relevant Web pages.
   • Check Vocabula Review's website at vocabula.com/VRlinks.htm to locate magazines, journals, and news sources that can be helpful.
   • Visit findarticles.com to locate magazine articles about your topic.

"I don't know how to end."

Imagine that you go to the movies and pay eight dollars to see the latest action film. The beginning is wonderful—you're on the edge of your seat. The middle is very exciting—you're completely caught up in the plot. Then the ending comes—and it's awful. When you walk out of the theater, you probably do not talk about how good the beginning and middle were. Instead, you probably complain about how bad the ending was. Why? Because endings form the last impression a person has, the one that is most remembered.

Your conclusion forms your reader's final impression. If your ending is weak, no matter how strong the rest of your writing is, your reader will feel let down. If you have trouble ending your writing, try the strategies in this chapter.

Troubleshooting Strategies

78 ✦ Explain the Significance of Your Main Point

Ideas in the conclusion are emphasized because of their placement at the end, where they are most likely to be remembered. Therefore, the conclusion can be a good place to state the significance of your point. For example, say you are telling the story of the time you were cut from the junior high basketball team. Your conclusion can explain the significance of the event:

Because being cut from the team shattered my self-esteem at such a young age, I have struggled all my life with feelings of inadequacy. I have doubted my ability because the coach, whose judgment I trusted, told me that I didn't have what it takes.

79 ← *Provide a Helpful Summary*

Summarizing your main points is a service to your reader if you have written a long essay or one with complex ideas. After reading a long or complicated piece of writing, a reader appreciates a review. However, if your essay is short or if the ideas are easily grasped, a summary would be a boring rehash of previously covered material.

80 ← *Explain the Consequences of Ignoring Your Thesis*

If you are writing to persuade your reader to think or act in a certain way, you can close by explaining what would happen if your reader did not follow your recommendation.

Assume, for example, that you are writing to convince your reader that a drug education program should be instituted in the local elementary school. After giving your reasons, you could close like this:

If we do not have a drug education program in the earliest grades, we miss the opportunity to influence our children when they are the most impressionable. If we miss this opportunity to influence them when they are young and responsive to adult pressure, we run the risk of losing our children to the powerful peer pressure to experiment with drugs.

81 ← *End with a Point You Want to Emphasize*

Anything placed at the end of your writing is emphasized. Therefore, you can conclude with your most important point, the one you want underscored in your reader's mind. For example, if you are explaining the differences between child-rearing practices of today and those of fifty years ago, you could end like this:

The most telling difference between child-rearing practices of today and those of fifty years ago is that today's parents are less rigid. Unlike the par-

ents of fifty years ago, they are less concerned with doing everything on sched-ule and by the book. Babies are not forced to eat and sleep at specific times but may do so when they are hungry and sleepy. Today's parents trust their instincts more than they trust the child-care book used by parents of the past. Thus, they are more likely to do what they think is right and not worry about what the authorities say.

82 ← Restate Your Thesis for Emphasis

Repetition is effective for judicious emphasis, but repetition is boring and annoying if it is unnecessary. Thus, if you decide to close by restating your thesis, be sure the restatement is effective emphasis rather than boring rep-etition. Also, avoid restating in the same language you used previously. Restate the thesis a *new* way.

83 ← Suggest a Course of Action

You can conclude by stating a remedy to a problem your essay discusses, or by calling your reader to action. For example, if you are writing about the reason for declining enrollment at your local public school, you can suggest a course of action in the conclusion:

The reasons for our declining enrollment are complex, but the solution to the problem is clear. First, we should hire a recruitment specialist and charge that person with aggressively seeking new students. At the same time, we should begin a marketing campaign, complete with local television and radio spots, to attract area people so they attend school here rather than out of state. Finally, we should hire a marketing firm to discover what potential students are seeking and try to meet those desires. Yes, these measures are expensive, but the money will be well spent if we can return enrollment figures to their previous high levels.

84 ← *Ask a Question*

You can leave your reader thinking about your thesis if you close with a suitable question. Take, for example, the following conclusion for a letter to the editor arguing against raising the speed limit on state routes:

> *If the speed limit is raised, truckers would save money, as would those who ship their goods on trucks. And while studies do not support the contention that the higher speed limit will mean more accidents, they suggest that the accidents that do occur would involve more fatalities. Do we really want to save money but lose lives?*

85 ← *Look to the Future*

Sometimes you can close effectively by looking ahead to a time beyond your writing. Say you are explaining the benefits and drawbacks of purchasing goods on the Internet. You could close by looking to the future, like this:

> *Although e-commerce has become increasingly popular over the last five years, the next five years will show a marked decline as people return to traditional stores. The novelty of online shopping will wear off as consumers admit to the difficulties of shopping for clothing and gifts they cannot touch, try on, and examine firsthand. Increased shipping costs will render online shopping too expensive, and fears about electronic security breaches (reasonable or not) will deter many consumers. Finally, consumers often miss the social and recreational aspects of shopping and will return to traditional stores for the simple human interaction they offer.*

86 ← *Combine Approaches*

You can combine any two or more approaches to create a strong finish. For example, you can summarize main points and then make a recommendation, or you can restate your thesis and then ask a question.

87 ← *Keep It Short*

If you have trouble with your conclusion, keep it short. Although you do not want to end abruptly, do not take something that is a problem and stretch it out longer than necessary. A perfectly effective ending can be only one or two sentences.

88 ← *Use a Computer to Help Find the Perfect Ending*

You can try the following strategies if you compose at the computer:

Use E-Mail. E-mail your draft *without* a conclusion to three reliable readers, and ask each one what he or she suggests for an approach to the ending. You might like one or more of the ideas.

Divide Your Screen. Divide your screen in half, and write two endings. Use two different approaches, each in its own screen. Compare the two approaches and decide which works better.

Use the Internet. George Mason University's Writing Center offers an online handout on introductions and conclusions that explains concluding strategies writers should avoid: gmu.edu/departments/writingcenter/handouts/introcon.html.

8

"I can't think of the right word."

You're writing along, and just as your confidence begins to surge— wham! You're stuck because you can't think of the right word. You try all the usual techniques—chewing on the end of your pencil to squeeze the word into the tip, rubbing your forehead to massage the word into your brain, and staring at the computer screen to will the word to appear—but nothing helps. Soon it's a matter of pride, and you refuse to budge until you think of the word that's lurking annoyingly just at the tip of your tongue. The next thing you know, fifteen minutes have passed, you have made no progress, and you are frustrated.

The next time the word you need escapes you, avoid frustration with the techniques in this chapter.

Troubleshooting Strategies

89 ← *Write in a Natural Style*

You may be straining for an overly "sophisticated" style, a style you think will impress the reader. As a result, words escape you because you are seeking ones that were never a natural part of your vocabulary in the first place. Return to a more natural style, and words should come more easily.

Unnatural:	Attempting to ruminate her morning nourishment while simultaneously communicating the events that transpired, Emma began to choke on her victuals.
More natural:	Trying to tell what happened at the same time she was eating breakfast, Emma began to choke.

90 ← *Use ITTS*

ITTS stands for "*I'm trying to say.*" When you cannot find the right word, stop for a moment and say to yourself, "I'm trying to say _____." Imagine yourself explaining what you mean to a friend, and fill in the blank with the word or words you would speak to that friend. Then write the word or words in your draft. You may use several words or even a sentence to fill in the blank when originally you were only seeking a single word. That's fine.

91 ← *Substitute a Phrase or a Sentence for a Troublesome Word*

If you cannot take one path, then take an alternate route to your destination. If you cannot think of the right word, try using a phrase or a whole sentence to express your idea instead.

92 ← *Ask Around*

If you cannot think of the word that is on the tip of your tongue, then ask around. To anyone who will listen, just say, "Hey, what's the word for _____?" Writers are always glad to help each other.

93 ← *Freewrite for Three Minutes*

You may not be able to think of the right word because you are not certain about what you want to say. To clarify your thinking, try three minutes of freewriting, focusing on the idea you want the word to convey. (Freewriting is explained in Chapter 1.) After the freewriting, try again to come up with the word. You may find you can do so when you have a better understanding of what you want to express.

94 ← *Skip the Problem, and Return to It Later*

When you are drafting, never let any trouble spot prevent your progress. If after a minute you cannot think of the right word, then leave a blank space and push on. You can return to consider the problem again when you revise. When you return, the word may surface, and the problem will be solved. If not, you can try the other strategies in this chapter.

95 ↞ *Use Simple, Specific Words*

Some people have trouble finding the right words because they think good writing uses words like *bumptious, egregious, panacea, parsimonious,* and *pusillanimous.*

The truth is that good writing is clear, simple, and specific. You do not need the high-flown, fifty-dollar words. Instead of *parsimonious,* use *stingy.*

96 ↞ *Use the Thesaurus and Dictionary Wisely*

The thesaurus and dictionary are excellent tools for writers seeking the right word. In fact, you may want to invest in a hardback and paperback version of each of these resources. Keep the hardbacks on your writing desk, and carry the paperbacks around with you. A word of caution: be sure you understand the connotation (secondary meaning) of any word you draw from these sources. For example, *skinny* and *lean* may mean the same thing on one level, but because of their connotations, a person would rather be called *lean* than *skinny.* If you do not understand the connotations of a word, you can misuse it or offend your reader.

97 ↞ *Use a Computer to Help You Find the Right Words*

Try the following strategies if you compose at the computer.

Use a Thesaurus Program. Many word-processing programs come with a built-in thesaurus, or you can purchase an add-on thesaurus. Such a program can be handy, but be sure you understand the meaning of any word you take from this source.

Learn a Word a Day. Visit one of these websites to have a new word and its meaning e-mailed to you each day:

- wordsmith.org

- vocabvitamins.com

- m-w.com

Use the Internet. Expand your choice of words by trying the following websites:

- If you like visual representations, check out the Visual Thesaurus at visualthesaurus.com/online/index.jsp. This website uses maps to show the relationships between words and meanings.
- For an online thesaurus, you can visit the Merriam-Webster website at m-w.com.
- *Take Our Word for It* is a webzine about words. To see what it offers, visit takeourword.com.
- For help with vocabulary building, visit wordfocus.com.

PART 3

A Troubleshooting Guide to Revising

First drafts *always* have problems—that's why they are also called **rough drafts**. However, even the most troubled first draft gives you material to shape, refine, and improve. When you evaluate your first draft to determine what to change and when you make those changes, you are **revising**. To revise, consider your content, organization, and expression of ideas. Do not worry about grammar, spelling, capitalization, or punctuation just yet.

9

"I thought my draft was better than this."

Y ou've just placed the final period at the end of the last sentence of your first draft, and you're feeling proud of yourself. So you lean back, put your feet up on the desk, and start to reread the masterpiece. As you read, however, your masterpiece doesn't seem nearly as good as you thought it was. Does this mean you have to start over? Probably not. Instead, try some of the suggestions in this chapter.

Troubleshooting Strategies

98 ← *Be Realistic*
Remember, a first draft is called a *rough* draft because your first attempt is supposed to have problems—even lots of them. Do not expect too much too soon. Instead, realize your first pass is bound to be rough, roll up your sleeves, and get in there and revise.

99 ← *Walk Away*
Before deciding about the quality of your draft, put it aside for a while to regain your objectivity. The longer you stay away, the better; but walk away for at least several hours—for a day if you have the time. When you return to your draft and reread it, you may discover potential that you overlooked previously.

100 ← *Share Your Draft*

Sometimes writers are too hard on themselves. Instead of recognizing the potential in their drafts, they see only the rough spots. As a result, they become frustrated and start over unnecessarily. Before deciding about the quality of your draft, share it with several people whose judgment you trust. Ask what they like and what they want to hear more about. Your readers' comments may reveal how much potential your draft has. (For more on reader response, see Chapter 11.)

101 ← *Listen to Your Draft*

Your draft may seem worse than it is if it is messy, written in sloppy handwriting, written in pencil, or written on paper ripped out of a spiral notebook. In short, the appearance of the draft may affect your evaluation of it. To judge the worth of your draft more reliably, ask someone to read it to you. You may hear sections that are stronger than you realized.

102 ← *Identify Two Changes That Will Improve Your Draft*

Identify two changes that will make your draft better, and you may recognize how much potential your draft has. If you think it will help you judge your draft better, make those changes and *then* decide how you feel about your draft.

103 ← *Write a Second Draft Without Looking at the First*

Writing a second draft without looking at the first is often successful because you manage to retain the best parts of the first draft, eliminate the weakest parts, and add some new, effective material. The key is to avoid checking the first draft while writing the second.

104 ← *Do Not Despair if You Must Start Over*

Often we must discover what we do *not* want to do before we discover what we *do* want to do; sometimes we must learn what we *cannot* do before we are clear about what we *can* do. If you must begin again, do not be discouraged. Your first draft was not a waste of your time—it was groundwork that paved the way for your most recent effort.

105 ← *Try to Salvage Something*

If you must begin again, try to salvage something. Perhaps you can use the same approach to your introduction, or some of your examples, or one main idea. While it is tempting to rip the draft to shreds and begin anew, you may not have to begin at square one. Some of your work may be usable in your new draft.

106 ← *Do the Best You Can with What You Have*

Yes, writers start over all the time, but writers do not usually have an unlimited amount of time to work within. At some point, you must force yourself to push forward, even if you are not completely comfortable with the status of your first draft. When time is running out, do the best you can with what you have and be satisfied that you have met your deadline.

107 ← *Use a Computer to Help the Revision Process*

Computers can help writers revise efficiently. Consider the following strategies.

Evaluate a Print Copy of Your Draft. Computer screens display a small portion of your draft, making it hard to get a good overview. To decide about the strengths and weaknesses of your draft, print out a copy and read that.

Save Your Scraps. You may be tempted to hit the delete key, especially if you decide to start over, but resist the impulse. In a separate "scraps" file, save your first draft and any material you decide to omit. If you change your mind later and want to use the material, you will have it. If you are using Microsoft Word, you can save every version of your draft by clicking on "File" in the menu bar and then "Versions."

Use the Internet. For some questions to help you evaluate your draft, visit the Paradigm Online Writing Assistant at powa.org. Click on "Revising."

10

"I don't know what to change."

Good news! You finished your first draft, and you are ready to dig in and make all those changes that will improve your writing. So you read your draft—but wait a minute, everything seems fine. *You* understand what you mean; everything seems clear and well developed to you. In fact, you can't figure out what changes to make and what all the revision fuss is about. The suggestions in this chapter can help.

Troubleshooting Strategies

108 ← *Walk Away*

Before revising, put your draft aside for a day or longer if possible. Getting away from your writing gives you a chance to regain your objectivity so that when you return to revise, you can identify necessary changes more readily.

109 ← *Construct a Reader Profile*

As the writer, you may have no trouble figuring out what you meant when you wrote all those words, but that does not guarantee that your reader will have an easy time of it. To revise successfully, view your draft as a reader would, and make changes to meet your reader's needs. Different readers will place different demands on a writer. For example, assume you are writing to convince your reader to vote for a school levy that will increase property taxes. If your audience is someone with children in the school system, explaining that the additional revenue will go toward enhancing the art and music curriculum may be sufficiently persuasive. If, however, your reader is a childless retired person on a fixed income, this argument may not be very convincing. Instead, you may need to explain that better schools will cause the reader's home to increase in value so the resale price becomes higher.

To evaluate your detail from your reader's point of view, construct a reader profile by answering the following ten questions:

1. How much education does my reader have?

2. What are my reader's age, sex, race, nationality, and religion?

3. What are my reader's occupation and socioeconomic level?

4. What part of the country does my reader live in? Does my reader live in an urban or rural area?

5. What is my reader's political affiliation?

6. How familiar is my reader with my topic?

7. What does my reader need to know to appreciate my point of view?

8. How resistant will my reader be to my point of view?

9. How hard will I have to work to create interest in my topic?

10. Does my reader have any special hobbies, interests, or concerns that will affect how my essay is viewed? Is my reader chiefly concerned with money? career? the environment? society? religion? family?

After answering these questions, review your draft with an eye toward providing details suited to your reader's unique makeup.

110 ← *Think Like Your Reader*

Asking the following questions as you study your draft can help you think like your reader and identify necessary changes:

- Is there any place where my reader might lose interest?

- Is there any place where my reader might not understand what I mean?

- Is there any place where my reader is not likely to be convinced of the truth of my topic sentence or thesis?

111 ← *Describe Your Draft Paragraph by Paragraph*

Describing your draft paragraph by paragraph can help you analyze its strengths and weaknesses. To do this, summarize the content of the first paragraph; then explain how that paragraph meets your audience's needs and how it helps you achieve your purpose for writing. Next, summarize the content of the second paragraph; then explain how that paragraph meets your audience's needs and your purpose. Continue in this fashion until you have described each paragraph. Read your descriptions to identify points that stray from your thesis, ideas that need more development, and paragraphs that fail to meet a reader's needs or your purpose.

112 ← *Type Your Draft*

If you handwrote your draft, type it, print it out, and read it over. Problems you overlook in your own handwriting are more apparent in type because the copy resembles printed material rather than your own handiwork. As a result, it can be easier to be objective about the writing. Also, some mistakes may leap out at you. For example, a paragraph that ran the better part of a page in your handwritten copy may turn out to be only three typed lines—a visual signal that more detail may be needed.

113 ← *Listen to Your Draft*

Often, you can hear problems that you overlook visually. For this reason, you should read your draft out loud at least once. Be sure to go slowly, and be careful to read *exactly* what is on the page. If you read quickly, you are likely to read what you *meant* to write rather than what you actually *did* write.

Some writers do well if they read their drafts into a recorder. Then they play back the recording to listen for problems. Still other writers prefer to have other people read their drafts to them. Sometimes, another person's voice helps the writer pick up on problems.

114 ← *Underline Main Points*

One way to determine if you have supported your points is to go through your draft and underline every main idea. Then check to see what appears after each underlined point. If one underlined point is immediately followed by another underlined point, you have not supported a main idea. Similarly, if an underlined idea is followed by only one or two sentences, you should consider whether you have enough support. For strategies for supporting points, see Chapter 6.

115 ← *Outline Your Draft After Writing It*

A good way to determine if your ideas follow logically one to the next is to outline your draft *after* writing it. If you have points that do not fit into the outline at the appropriate spots, you have discovered an organization problem.

116 ← *Revise in Stages*

When you revise, you have a great deal to consider. To consider it all, revise in stages, using one of the following patterns:

• **Easy to hard.** First make all the easy changes, take a break, and then make the more difficult changes. Take a break whenever you become tired or when you get stuck. Making the easy changes first helps you build enough momentum to carry you through the harder changes.

• **Hard to easy.** Make some of your more difficult changes, take a break, make some more of your difficult changes, take another break, and continue with the harder changes, taking breaks as needed. When you have finished the more difficult changes, tackle the easier ones. Some writers like the psychological lift that comes from getting the hard changes out of the way.

• **Paragraph by paragraph.** Revise your first paragraph until it is as perfect as you can make it, and then go on to the next paragraph. Proceed paragraph by paragraph, taking a break after every paragraph or two.

• **Content, organization, effective expression.** First make all your content changes: adequate detail, relevant detail, specific detail, clarity, and suitable introduction and conclusion. Then take a break and check the organization: logical order of ideas, effective thesis, and clear topic sentences. Take another break and revise for sentence effectiveness: effective word choice, smooth flow, and helpful transitions.

117 ✦ *Share Your Opening and Closing*

To judge the effectiveness of your opening and closing, type up these parts separately, and give them to two or three people to read. Ask them whether they would be interested in reading something with that beginning and ending.

118 ✦ *Share Your Draft*

To help them decide what and how to revise, writers often ask reliable readers to read their drafts and make suggestions. If you want to consider the opinions of readers when you make revision decisions, refer to the strategies in Chapter 11.

119 ✦ *Pretend to Be Someone Else*

To be more objective about your work, pretend you are someone else. Read your draft as the judge of a contest who will award you $10,000 for a prizewinning essay. Or become the editor of a magazine who is deciding what changes to make in the draft before publishing the piece. Or read it as your worst enemy, someone who loves to find fault with your work.

120 ← *Use a Revising Checklist*

Some writers like to use a revising checklist such as the following one. The checklist keeps you from overlooking some of the revision concerns. In addition, you can combine this checklist with reader responses by asking a reliable reader to apply the checklist to your draft. (The chapters in parentheses refer you to the relevant parts of this book.)

Content

1. Does your writing have a clear thesis, either stated or implied, that accurately presents your focus? (Chapter 2)

2. Are all your main points, including your thesis, adequately supported? (Chapter 6)

3. Have you avoided stating the obvious? (Chapter 15)

4. Does your opening create interest in your topic? (Chapter 5)

5. Does your conclusion provide a satisfying ending? (Chapter 7)

Organization

1. Do your ideas follow logically one to the next? (Chapter 12)

2. Do your paragraphs follow logically one to the next? (Chapter 12)

3. Have you used transitions to show how ideas relate to each other? (Chapter 12)

Expression

1. When you read your work aloud, does everything sound all right? (Chapter 9)

2. Have you avoided wordiness? (Chapter 14)

3. Have you eliminated clichés (overworked expressions)? (Chapter 15)

4. Have you used specific words? (Chapter 15)

5. Did you use a variety of sentence openers? (Chapter 16)

6. Have you used the active voice? (Chapter 15)

7. Have you used action verbs rather than forms of *be*? (Chapter 15)

8. Have you used parallel structures? (Chapter 16)

121 ✦ *Trust Your Instincts*

When your instincts tell you that something is wrong, assume you have a problem. Even if you cannot give the problem a name, and even if you are not yet sure what change should be made, you have identified something that needs to be reworked. Most of the time, a writer's instincts are correct.

122 ✦ *Do Not Edit Prematurely*

Sometimes writers have trouble deciding what to change because they get bogged down checking commas, spelling, fragments, and the like. Concerns such as these, however, are matters of correctness and are best dealt with later, during editing. During revision, focus on content, organization, and effective expression. Do not be distracted by editing concerns too early in the writing process.

123 ✦ *Use a Computer to Help You Decide What to Revise*

If you revise at the computer, consider the following tips.

Study a Print Copy of Your Draft. When you view the text on the screen, you see small portions at a time, so you don't get a good overview of your writing.

Do Not Be Fooled by Appearances. Word-processed material looks very professional because it is so neat and well formatted. Do not let the appearance of your draft fool you into thinking that no changes are needed.

Use the Find-and-Replace Command. If you tend to overuse certain words, use Microsoft Word's find-and-replace command to check how many times you have used those words. For example, if you overuse *very*, type "very" into *both* the "Find" and "Replace" boxes. Then click on "Replace All," and Microsoft Word will count the number of times you have used that word to help you judge whether you have used it too much. (Nothing will be replaced.)

Keep Your Reader Profile and Revision Checklist as Files. If you keep your reader profile and revision checklist as files, you can consult them each time you revise. If your computer allows you to split your screen, place the checklist or profile in a window to refer to as you revise.

Use the Internet. For helpful information on how to revise, visit this University of Texas Web page: utexas.edu/student/utlc/handouts/1234 .html.

11

"What if I want some constructive criticism?"

Getting constructive criticism can be a crucial part of the writing process. That's why you so often hear a writer say, "Read this and tell me what you think." Because the opinion of readers is so valuable to writers, this chapter explains strategies for securing helpful reader response.

Troubleshooting Strategies

124 ✦ *Choose Your Readers Carefully*
Be sure the people who read your work know the qualities of effective writing. A person who rarely reads or writes may not be a good choice. Also be sure that your readers are comfortable giving constructive criticism; do not use someone who is reluctant to tell you if something is wrong.

125 ✦ *Give Your Readers a Legible Draft*
Make your reader's job as easy as possible. If necessary, print out or write a fresh, clear copy of your draft so your reader can easily read your work.

126 ← *Give Your Readers Guidance*

If you have specific concerns about your draft, mention them and ask your readers to respond to those points. As an alternative, give your readers a questionnaire like this one:

1. Can you easily tell what the thesis (focus) of my writing is? If so, what is it?

2. Are you interested in reading about this? Why or why not?

3. What do you like best about this writing?

4. Do any points go unproven or unsupported? If so, which ones?

5. Is there anything you do not understand? If so, what?

6. Does the order of ideas make sense? If not, explain the problem.

7. Does any detail stray from my focus? If so, what?

8. Does the opening engage your interest? Why or why not?

9. Is the ending satisfying? Why or why not?

10. What advice do you have that was not covered by the previous questions?

127 ← *Get More than One Opinion*

Ask two or three reliable readers to respond to your draft, and then look for consensus. When multiple readers agree, chances are they are right. If a reader makes a comment you are unsure about, ask another reader to respond to that same point so you can have another opinion.

128 ← *Ask for Specific Revision Strategies*

Readers should do more than point out problems; they should also suggest ways to solve those problems. Instead of "Paragraph 2 needs detail," a reader should say, "Paragraph 2 needs more detail. Perhaps you could add two examples of how schools reward conformity."

129 ← *Ask Readers to Point Out Strengths as Well as Weaknesses*

To revise effectively, you need a sense of your draft's strengths *and* weaknesses, so ask your readers what they like best about your draft and why.

130 ← *Evaluate Responses Carefully*

Do not assume your readers are always correct. Weigh out their responses carefully. If you need clarification, ask your readers why they responded as they did.

131 ← *Use a Computer to Get Some Constructive Criticism*

If you like to compose and revise at the computer, you may like the next strategies.

E-Mail Your Draft. E-mail your draft to reliable readers to secure their reactions. If you want them to respond to particular sections of the draft, boldface those sections and ask your readers to pay particular attention to those parts. Many word-processing programs allow inserting comments on the draft. For Microsoft Word, highlight the text to comment on, click "Insert" on the menu bar and then "Comment." A window appears with comments that have already been made and the name or initials of the person who made the comment. Type your comments next to your name or initials and click on "Close." Highlighting on the draft will signal that a comment has been made.

Use the Internet. For information on how to give useful feedback to other writers, see the University of Wisconsin–Madison's website at wisc .edu/writing/Handbook/PeerReviews.html.

12

"My ideas seem all mixed up."

Let's say you finish your draft, and you're feeling confident until you read it over—or a reliable reader does—and discover that your ideas do not seem connected to each other. Everything is a jumble. Does this mean your ideas are no good? Absolutely not. It means that when you revise, you should use the suggestions in this chapter to better organize your writing.

Troubleshooting Strategies

132 ← Write a Postdraft Outline

To check the organization, you can outline your draft *after* it is written. To do this, fill in an outline map, outline tree, or formal outline with the ideas already written in your draft (see Chapter 3). If you discover points that do not fit logically into a particular section of the outline, you have an organization problem that needs your attention.

133 ← Use Transitions

Transitions are words and phrases that show how ideas relate to each other. Sometimes when your ideas seem mixed up, you just need to supply appropriate transitions to make the connections between points more explicit. Consider these sentences:

Today's economy is not good for the stock market. There is still money to be made in speculative stocks.

Without a transitional word or phrase, the reader will not see how the ideas in the two sentences relate to each other. Add a transition to solve this problem:

Today's economy is not good for the stock market. <u>Nevertheless</u>, there is still money to be made in speculative stocks.

The following transitions can help you demonstrate how your ideas relate to each other:

also	in like fashion
although	in other words
and	in short
as a result	in summary
at the same time	in the same way
consequently	later
earlier	moreover
even though	near
for example	nevertheless
for instance	now
for this reason	on the contrary
furthermore	on the other hand
however	similarly
in addition	then
in conclusion	therefore
indeed	thus
in fact	yet
in front of	

134 ← *Repeat Key Words*

You can often show how ideas relate to each other by repeating a key word or words, like this:

The Senate is scheduled to vote on the tax reform <u>bill</u> Wednesday. This <u>bill</u> will reduce taxes.

135 ← *Use Synonyms*

You can also demonstrate how ideas relate to each other by using synonyms to repeat a key idea, like this:

> *The Senate is scheduled to vote on the tax reform <u>bill</u> Wednesday. This <u>leg-islation</u> will reduce taxes.*

136 ← *Use Outline Cards*

Write your thesis and each of your main ideas on separate index cards. To experiment with alternate orders, arrange and rearrange the cards until your ideas progress in the best order.

137 ← *Use a Computer to Help Order Your Ideas*

If your ideas seem mixed up, the computer can provide assistance.

Copy and Rearrange Your Draft. Make a copy of your draft in a new file. Then use the cut-and-paste functions to try your paragraphs in a new order.

Boldface Your Thesis and Main Ideas. Check every boldfaced topic sentence against your thesis to be sure each is clearly related. Then check every sentence in your body paragraphs to be sure each is relevant to its boldfaced main idea. If an idea is not relevant, delete it or revise to make it relevant.

Make a Postdraft Outline. Save your draft. Then create a copy of the draft in a new file. Reduce this copy to an outline by identifying in each paragraph the major idea and the major supporting details; strip everything else from each paragraph (using the delete key or a block erase), leaving just the sentences that give the main ideas and major supporting details.

Next, identify your thesis sentence and write it at the top of your outline. Now use Roman and Arabic numerals, as well as capital and lower-case letters, to sequence the remaining sentences following the thesis sentence into a formal outline. Study this outline and make any necessary adjustments.

Once you have made and adjusted the outline, you can place it in a window, then recall the original draft, and revise it according to the outline. Or you can print the outline and use it as a revision guide.

Use the Internet. To view an example of a formal outline, visit this Web page from the Lloyd Sealy Library of the City University of New York: lib.jjay.cuny.edu/research/outlining.html.

For information on writing effective transitions, visit the following page from the website of the Writing Center at the University of North Carolina at Chapel Hill: unc.edu/depts/wcweb/handouts/transitions.html.

13

"My draft is too short."

You think you have enough ideas to get under way, so you start drafting. Then you come to the end and place a period after your last sentence. You look back over your work and come to the disheartening recognition that your draft is much too short, and you have already said everything you can think of. What do you do? No, you do not throw yourself in front of a high-speed train. Instead, try one of the strategies in this chapter.

Troubleshooting Strategies

138 ✦ *Underline Major Points*

Underline every major point in your draft. Then check to see how much you have written after each underlined point. If one underlined point is immediately followed by another underlined point, you have neglected to develop an idea. Adding detail after one or more of your major points can solve your length problem. (See Chapter 6 for ways to add detail.)

When you add detail, do not state the obvious or provide unrelated information, or you will be guilty of padding—that is, writing useless material just to bulk up the piece. Padding irritates readers by requiring them to read unnecessary material.

Assume that you are explaining how schools foster competition, rather than cooperation, in students. If you say that schools have students compete for grades, compete for positions on sports teams, compete for student government, compete for scholarships, and compete for cheerleading, you would be providing helpful examples to illustrate your point. However, if you give a dictionary definition of *competition* as "the act of struggling to win some prize, honor, or advantage," you would be padding your essay with information your reader already knows.

139 ← *Show After You Tell*

If your draft is too short, you may be *telling* your reader things are true without *showing* that they are true. Remember to "show, don't just tell." Consider the following:

> *I have always hated winter. For one thing, the cold bothers me. For another, daily living becomes too difficult.*

The previous sentences are an example of telling without showing. Here is a revision with detail added to *show*:

> *I have always hated winter. For one thing, the cold bothers me. Even in the house with the furnace running, I can never seem to get warm. I wear a turtleneck under a heavy wool sweater and drink one cup of hot tea after another in a futile effort to ease the chill that goes to my bones. A simple trip to the mailbox at the street leaves me chattering for an hour. My hands go numb, and my nose and ears sting from the cold. The doctor explained that I cannot tolerate the cold because I have a circulation problem, which causes my capillaries to spasm, interrupting the blood flow to my extremities. I also hate winter because daily living becomes too difficult. Snow and ice are tracked into the house, necessitating frequent cleanups. Snow must be shoveled to get the car out of the driveway. Icy walks make walking treacherous, and driving to the grocery store becomes a dangerous endeavor thanks to slick, snow-covered roads.*

140 ← *Add Description*

Description can add interest and liveliness, and it can help your reader form clear mental images. To flesh out an essay, look for opportunities to describe a person or scene. For more on description, see Chapter 6.

141 ← *Add Examples*

Examples clarify matters and make things more specific. As you work to lengthen a draft, look for general statements that can be illustrated with a well-chosen example or two. For more on examples, see Chapter 6.

142 ← *Add Dialogue*

Sometimes you can enliven an essay by adding the words that were spoken. Consider the following paragraph:

> *I stepped up to the plate, ready to swing away, but the catcher kept saying things to shake my confidence. I tried to ignore him and keep my focus, but the next thing I knew, I was too nervous to swing at all. The pitcher threw three pitches, the umpire called three strikes, and I walked to the outfield feeling like a fool.*

Notice, now, how much more full-bodied the paragraph is with the addition of dialogue:

> *I stepped up to the plate, ready to swing away, but the catcher kept saying things to shake my confidence. "I hope you don't choke like the last time," he sneered as I tapped the bat against the inside of my shoe. "Move in; easy out," he shouted to the outfield as I assumed my batting stance. I tried to ignore him and keep my focus, but the next thing I knew, I was too nervous to swing at all. "I figured you'd choke, you big baby," he sneered after the first called strike. The pitcher threw three pitches, the umpire called three strikes, and I walked to the outfield feeling like a fool.*

143 ← *Evaluate the Significance of an Idea*

In addition to stating an idea, explain its importance, impact, or meaning. For example, assume you are arguing that the proposed site for the new state prison on the north end of town is not a good choice. You could explain the significance of the choice of site:

The proposed site on the north end of town is favored by state legislators, not because it is inherently the best site, but because their wealthy campaign contributors want the building as far away from their residences as possible. The legislators fear angering their wealthy supporters because they do not want to lose financial assistance from these supporters in future campaigns.

144 ↤ Share Your Draft with a Reliable Reader

Ask someone with good judgment about writing to review your draft and suggest where and what kind of detail is needed. For a detailed discussion of using a reliable reader, see Chapter 11.

145 ↤ Return to Idea Generation

Your draft may be too short because you began writing before you generated enough ideas to write about. If you have a favorite idea-generation technique, try it now. If it lets you down, try one or more of the other techniques described in Chapter 1.

146 ↤ Check Your Thesis

Study your thesis to see if it too severely limits the territory you can cover. If so, broaden the thesis a bit so you can cover more ground and thereby increase the length of your draft. Let's say your draft has this thesis:

High school athletics teaches adolescents to be self-reliant.

If you have exhausted everything you can say about how high school athletics teaches self-reliance, and you have tried all the techniques in this chapter, consider expanding your thesis to allow discussion of other points:

High school athletics teaches adolescents to be self-reliant. Interestingly, however, athletics also teaches young people how to be team players.

Now you can expand the draft by discussing two advantages of high school athletics rather than one.

A word of caution is in order here: do not get carried away when you expand your thesis, or you will be forced into covering too much territory. Consider how difficult it would be to provide an adequately detailed discussion of this expanded thesis:

High school athletics teaches adolescents everything they need to know to succeed as adults: how to be self-reliant, how to be a team player, how to function under pressure, how to accept criticism, and how to give 100 percent.

A piece of writing with this thesis will fail in one of two ways. Either the writing will be so long that the reader will feel overwhelmed, or it will provide only superficial treatment of the main points.

147 ✦ *Use a Computer to Help You Lengthen Your Draft*

The following computer strategies can help you lengthen a draft.

Separate Main Points and Explanatory Details. Before each of your main points, press the insert key and hit the space bar five times to create a visual separation between each main point and its explanatory details. The separation will help you study each point and its support individually to determine if you can add an example, story, dialogue, or description. After making your additions, rejoin your sentences to form a longer draft.

Count Your Words. Many programs allow you to do a word count. If you are using Microsoft Word, click on "Tools" in the menu bar and then "Word Count" to determine how close you are to your desired or optimal length. You can also highlight an individual paragraph to count its words if you like.

Use the Internet. Examples are an excellent way to clarify points and add details. Visit the Capital Community College website for helpful information on using examples at ccc.commnet.edu/grammar/composition /examples.htm.

14

"My draft is too long."

Perhaps you are inspired and write page after page after page after page—all the while feeling great because you have so much to say. Unfortunately, longer is not necessarily better. Your reader's time is valuable, so keep your writing to a length that will not unduly tax your audience. If your draft is too long, try the strategies given here.

Troubleshooting Strategies

148 ✦ *Check Your Thesis*

Look for ways to narrow the scope of your thesis. If your thesis spreads over too much territory, you will be forced to cover too many points, and the result will be a very long piece of writing. Consider this thesis:

The amount of violence on television, in the movies, and in popular fiction is alarming.

To discuss television, movie, and book violence in adequate detail would require many, many pages. A more manageable piece of writing would result from a thesis like this:

The amount of violence in prime-time network television is alarming.

149 ← *Eliminate Unnecessary Points*

Be sure you are not making unnecessary points. For example, assume you are writing a report on the mutual funds that provide the best retirement income. If you are writing for your boss, who is an investment banker, it would be silly to define the term *mutual funds*. However, in a newspaper article for readers who may not know what mutual funds are, a definition would be helpful. Similarly, if you are comparing two kinds of bicycles, you should not mention that both have two tires, as this would be stating the obvious.

150 ← *Outline Your Draft*

Even if you outlined before drafting, outline your draft after you write it. Then check the outline to be sure you are not repeating points or including irrelevant details. Be sure all your details are relevant to both the topic and the assertion expressed in your thesis.

151 ← *Eliminate Wordiness*

Eliminate wordiness in the following ways:

1. Eliminate repetition.

Wordy: My biggest problem and concern was how to pay next month's rent. (Problem and concern are repetitious.)
Better: My biggest problem was how to pay next month's rent.
Better: My biggest concern was how to pay next month's rent.

2. Eliminate deadwood (words that add no meaning).

Deadwood	Better
the color green	green
mix together	mix
past history	past
end result	result
important essentials	essentials

Wordy: I cannot concentrate unless I am alone by myself.
Better: I cannot concentrate unless I am alone.
Better: I cannot concentrate unless I am by myself.

3. Pare down wordy phrases.

Wordy	Better
in this day and age	now
in society today	today
being that	since
due to the fact that	because
for the purpose of	so

Wordy: At this point in time, I do not think we can afford the rate increase.
Better: I do not think we can afford the rate increase now.

4. Reduce the number of phrases.

Wordy: The shortage of skilled labor in this country points to the need for a greater number of vocational education programs.
Better: This country's skilled labor shortage points to a needed increase in vocational education programs.

5. Reduce the number of "that" clauses.

Wordy: The reporters asked the senator to repeat the explanation that she gave earlier.
Better: The reporters asked the senator to repeat her earlier explanation.

152 ❦ *Do Not Overwrite Your Opening or Closing*

Check your opening and closing to be sure one or both are not overly long. Remember, these parts are meant only to pave the way for your main discussion and wrap things up at the end.

153 ← *Use a Computer to Help Shorten Your Draft*

The following suggestions can help you find ways to shorten a draft.

Separate Your Sentences. Hit the enter key after each sentence to reformat your writing into a list of sentences. With your sentences listed, you may find it easier to check them for wordiness.

Count Your Words. Highlight each paragraph separately, and use the word count feature to determine the number of words in each paragraph. If one paragraph is significantly longer than the others, check it for irrelevant detail.

Use the Find and Cut Functions. Use the find function to locate each of these words: *very, some, quite, so*. If you judge they should be cut, do so.

Use the Internet. To learn more about wordiness and how to eliminate it, visit the Purdue Writing Center website: http://owl.english.purdue.edu. Type "wordiness" into the search box.

15

"My writing seems boring."

"**I** couldn't put it down!" "A real page-turner!" "A must-read!" No, these are not the exclamations people must make about your writing, but you do have a responsibility to hold your reader's interest. If your draft seems boring, try the strategies described in this chapter to improve your detail and style.

Troubleshooting Strategies

154 ← *Replace General Words with Specific Ones*

To add interest, replace general words with more specific ones. Here are two sentences. The first has general words, which are underlined; the second has specific words, which are also underlined. Which sentence is more interesting?

> **General words:** The car went down the street.
> **Specific words:** The red Corvette streaked down Dover Avenue.

You probably found the second sentence more interesting because of its more specific word choice.

The following table will give you a clearer idea of the difference between general and specific words:

General	Specific
car	1989 Buick
dog	mangy collie
sweater	yellow cardigan

hat	Phillies cap
shoes	Nike Air Max
speak	mumble
feel good	feel optimistic
book	*Angela's Ashes*
walk	saunter
drink	slurp
cry	sob
loudly said	snapped
house	two-story colonial
rain	pounding rain
a lot	twelve
later	in two days

155 ← *Use Active Voice*

To give your writing more energy, rewrite sentences so that their subjects perform the actions indicated by the verbs. Then your sentences will be in the **active voice.** Here is an example:

The labor leader negotiated a new contract for the autoworkers. (The action suggested by the verb negotiated *is performed by the subject, "labor leader.")*

When the subject does not perform the verb's action (putting the sentence in the **passive voice**), the sentence has less energy:

The new contract for the autoworkers was negotiated by the labor leader. (The subject "the new contract" does not perform the action of the verb negotiated.*)*

156 ← *Substitute Action Verbs for Forms of* to Be

Forms of *to be* (e.g., *am, is, are, was, were*) have less energy and interest than action verbs. So when possible use action verbs, like this:

Less energy: Mayor Daley <u>was</u> always a believer in party politics.
More energy: Mayor Daley always <u>believed</u> in party politics.

157 ← *Rewrite Clichés*

Clichés are tired, overworked expressions. At one time, the expressions were fresh and interesting, but because of overuse, they have become boring. Here is a representative sampling of clichés:

cold as ice	hard as nails
free as a bird	under the weather
sadder but wiser	bull in a china shop
high as a kite	raining cats and dogs
last but not least	in the same boat
green with envy	the last straw
fresh as a daisy	smart as a whip
stiff as a board	

To add interest, replace clichés with more original phrasings:

Cliché: When the police officer pulled me over for speeding, I was <u>shaking like a leaf.</u>
Revision: When the police officer pulled me over for speeding, I was <u>trembling with anxiety.</u>

158 ← *Eliminate Obvious Statements*

Stating the obvious makes writing boring. Let's say you are arguing that young people should not be permitted to watch more than an hour of television a day. A sentence like the following will bore a reader, because some of what it says is so obvious it does not need to be said at all:

Television, an electronic device for bringing sound and pictures into the home, can be a positive or negative influence on our children, depending on how it is used.

To make your writing more interesting, eliminate obvious statements:

Television can influence our children for good or ill, depending on how it is used.

159 ↚ *Include Dialogue*

Including the words people have spoken is a good way to enliven writing—especially when you are telling a story—because dialogue adds interest and immediacy. For more on dialogue, see Chapter 13.

160 ↚ *Add Description*

Description adds vitality and interest, so look for opportunities to describe something: a scene, a person's clothing, a facial expression, a tone of voice, the brightness of the sun, the feel of a handshake. The description need not be elaborate, nor should it distract the reader from your main point. For example, if you are telling the story of a first encounter, some description can add liveliness:

The door was open, and I saw Dr. Harkness hunched over his desk, his nose on the paper he was studying, his eyes squinted into slits. I knocked on the door frame to get his attention, but the barely perceptible sound was too much for him. He jerked upright, startled by the intrusion. When he saw me, he brushed wisps of white hair from his eyes, smoothed his red and blue flannel shirt, and smiled sheepishly. "How can I help you, young man?" he asked, as he lifted his bulky frame from the chair.

161 ↚ *Add Examples*

Examples add interest because they are specific. Look for opportunities to follow a general point with an example. For instance, if you say that Lee is a scatterbrain, show this by giving the example of the day Lee locked the keys in the car three times.

162 ← *Tell a Story*

A brief story can add interest and help establish a point by serving as an example. For instance, assume you are explaining that being a student *and* a parent can get very complicated. Also assume that one point you make is that the two roles can conflict with each other. To establish this point, you could tell the story of the time your six-year-old woke up sick three hours before your history exam and you had to get her to the doctor, arrange for a babysitter, pick up a prescription—and still make it to class on time.

163 ← *Check Your Thesis*

If your thesis covers too much territory, you can be forced into a superficial, general discussion—and such discussions are boring. For example, consider this thesis:

> *Professional sports should be reformed.*

A piece of writing that adequately covers all professional sports and all areas that could benefit from reform is likely to involve a superficial discussion, because anything in-depth will lead to a very long piece. If your thesis is too ambitious, pare it down, like this:

> *During the off-season as well as the playing season, athletes should have to submit to random drug testing.*

Now you can provide a much more interesting discussion by giving specifics and still have a written piece of a manageable length.

164 ← *Use a Computer to Help Add Interest to Your Draft*

These following strategies can help you improve a boring draft.

Use the Find and Replace Functions. Use the find function to locate each of these general words: *very, quite, a lot, rather, really, great, good, bad,* and *some.* Evaluate each, and decide whether to revise for more specificity.

Use the Grammar Checker—Cautiously. If your word-processing program includes a grammar checker that flags problems, use it with caution, as these grammar checkers are not always reliable. Do not automatically assume that a flagged passage is really a problem—evaluate it yourself. Conversely, do not assume that unflagged passages are problem-free.

Use the Internet. The Purdue University Online Writing Lab has helpful information on active voice and passive voice. Visit it at http://owl.english.purdue.edu/handouts/print/grammar/g_actpass.html.

For an extensive compilation of clichés given alphabetically, visit cliche site.com.

16

"My writing sounds choppy."

Read this paragraph out loud. It sounds choppy. It does not flow. The style seems immature. It sounds like it was written by someone's kid brother. This is my way of showing that choppiness is bad. Is it working?

Actually, you do not always have to read your work aloud to detect choppiness. When you read silently, the words "sound" in your brain, allowing you to "hear" this problem. Then you can eliminate it with the techniques described in this chapter.

Troubleshooting Strategies

165 ← *Use Different Sentence Openers*

Writing sounds choppy when too many sentences in a row begin the same way. For example, the first paragraph of this chapter sounds choppy because most of the sentences begin with the subject. The solution is to mix the following sentence openings:

1. Open with a descriptive word (a *modifier*).

   <u>Strangely</u>, little Billy did not enjoy his birthday.
   <u>Confused</u>, the stranger asked directions to a bus stop.
   <u>Melting</u>, the ice formed slushy puddles on the pavement.

2. Open with a descriptive phrase (a *modifier*).

<u>Despite my better judgment</u>, I bought a ticket for the roller-coaster ride.

<u>Hiding in the living room</u>, twelve of us waited for the right moment to leap out and yell, "Surprise!"

<u>Pleased by her grade on the physics exam</u>, Loretta treated herself to a special dinner.

<u>Under the couch</u>, the wet dog hid from her owner.

3. Open with a *subordinate clause* (a dependent word group with a subject and verb).

<u>When Congress announced its budget reform package</u>, members of both political parties offered their support.

<u>If the basketball team can recruit a power forward</u>, we will have all the ingredients for a winning season.

<u>Before you contribute to a charity</u>, check the identification of the person requesting the money.

4. Open with *to* and the verb (an *infinitive*).

<u>To protect</u> our resources, we must all recycle.

<u>To convince</u> my parents to buy me a car, I had to agree to pay the car insurance.

<u>To gain</u> five pounds by the start of wrestling season, Luis doubled his intake of carbohydrates.

5. Open with the subject.

<u>Losses</u> led gains in today's stock market activity.

<u>Corvina's goal</u> is to become the youngest manager in the company's history.

<u>The curtains</u> were dulled by years of accumulated dirt.

166 ← *Vary the Placement of Transitions*

Transitions are words and phrases that link ideas and show how they relate to each other. (Transitions are discussed in Chapter 12.) One way to eliminate choppiness is to vary the placement of transitions.

Transition at the beginning:	In addition, providing child care in the workplace is a good idea because half of all mothers now work.
Transition in the middle:	Jan's opinion, on the other hand, is that child-care programs will cost too much.
Transition at the end:	Many employers now offer day care as a benefit, however.

167 ← *Combine Short Sentences*

When you hear choppiness, look to see if you have two or more short sentences in a row. If so, combine at least two of those short sentences into a longer one, using one of these words:

and	nor
because	or
but	so
for	yet

Short sentences (choppy):	The house was well constructed. It was decorated badly.
Combined sentence (smoother):	The house was well constructed, but it was decorated badly.
Short sentences (choppy):	The police and firefighters both needed money. They combined their resources in a fund-raiser.
Combined sentence (smoother):	The police and firefighters both needed money, so they combined their resources in a fund-raiser.

168 ← *Follow Long Sentences with Short Ones and Short Sentences with Long Ones*

The following examples alternate long and short sentences. As you read them, notice how well they flow.

Short followed by long: The coach jumped to his feet. Although he had been coaching for twenty years, he had never before seen such a perfectly executed play.

Long followed by short: This city needs a mayor who knows how to deal effectively with city council and how to trim waste from the municipal budget. This city needs Dale Davidson.

169 ← *Use Parallel Construction*

So sentences flow smoothly, keep series items **parallel** by putting them in the same grammatical form.

Not parallel: Coach Rico values teamwork, sportsmanship, and she values effort.

Parallel: Coach Rico values teamwork, sportsmanship, and effort.

Not parallel: The offensive television commercial insults women, glamorizes drinking, and it diminishes the importance of the family.

Parallel: The offensive television commercial insults women, glamorizes drinking, and diminishes the importance of the family.

170 ← *Use Your Ear*

Read your writing aloud with a pen in your hand. When you hear choppiness, place a check mark. Then go back and try the techniques described in this chapter to improve the flow of sentences.

171 ← *Use a Computer to Smooth Out Your Writing*
The following strategies can help you eliminate choppiness and improve the flow of your sentences.

Use the Grammar Checker—Cautiously. Your word-processing program's grammar checker will flag parallelism problems. However, grammar checker are not completely reliable, so do not assume that a flagged sentence has a problem—or that an unflagged sentence is satisfactory.

Use the Copy-and-Paste Function. You can vary the placement of some transitions by copying and pasting them at the beginning, middle, or end of a sentence—as needed.

Transition in the middle:	The solution, <u>therefore</u>, is to start a block watch and neighborhood intervention programs.
Copy *therefore*, and move it to the beginning:	<u>Therefore</u>, the solution is to start a block watch and neighborhood intervention programs.

Use the Internet. For additional information on parallelism and transitions, visit these University of Wisconsin–Madison writing center Web pages:

- wisc.edu/writing/Handbook/CommonErrors_Para.html

- wisc.edu/writing/Handbook/Transitions.html#addition

For information on sentence variety, visit the St. Cloud State website at http://leo.stcloudstate.edu/style/sentencev.html.

PART 4

A Troubleshooting Guide to Editing

Everyone—and I mean *everyone*—makes mistakes with grammar, spelling, punctuation, and capitalization. Frankly, there is nothing wrong with making mistakes—as long as *you* find and correct them before your *reader* does, in a process called **editing**. Editing is important because mistakes are distracting. Serious errors or frequent mistakes can also cause readers to lose confidence in your ability.

"I don't find my mistakes."

When your reader finds a mistake that you overlooked, do you smack yourself on the forehead and wonder, "How did I miss that?" You missed it because you didn't use editing strategies to help you find and correct errors. The techniques in this chapter and the ones that follow can solve that problem.

Troubleshooting Strategies

172 ↤ *Edit Last*
The time to **edit** (find and correct mistakes) is toward the end of your writing process. During idea generation, drafting, and revising, mistakes are not an issue, because you are focusing on content. If you edit during these stages, you may look up the spelling of a word that you eliminate during revision anyhow or check a comma in a sentence that never makes it to the final draft. Once done with revising, however, you can scrutinize your draft for errors.

173 ↤ *Leave Your Work for a While*
By the time you are ready to look for errors, you may not have a fresh enough perspective to notice mistakes. To compensate for this, you should leave your writing for a day to clear your head. When you return, you will have a sharper eye for spotting errors.

174 ↤ *Point to Each Word and Punctuation Mark*

Go over your writing very slowly. If you build up even a little speed, you can overlook errors because you will see what you *intended* to write rather than what you actually *did* write. You know so well what you want to say that you may see it on the page whether it is there or not. One way to ensure that you move slowly is to point to each word and punctuation mark and study each one a second or two. Read what you are pointing to; do not move your finger or pen ahead of what you are reading, or you will build up speed and miss mistakes.

175 ↤ *Use a Ruler*

Place a ruler under the first line of your writing, and examine that line for mistakes one word at a time. Then drop the ruler down a line and examine that line for mistakes. This way, you may have better luck finding errors—for two reasons. First, you are less likely to build up speed and miss mistakes. Second, the ruler prevents the words below the line from entering your visual field and distracting you.

176 ↤ *Prepare a Fresh, Word-Processed Copy*

Because handwriting can be hard on the eyes, errors can be spotted more easily in type. Also, you can be more objective about a word-processed copy because it seems more like printed materials—more like someone else's writing.

177 ↤ *Listen to Your Draft*

Sometimes you can hear mistakes that you overlook visually. Have someone read your draft to you, read it aloud to yourself, or speak it into a recorder and play it back. If you read your draft to yourself or into a recorder, be sure to read *exactly* what is on the page. Remember, writers tend to read what they *meant* to say rather than what they *did* say. Also, remember that some mistakes, such as certain misspellings, cannot be heard, so listening should be combined with visual editing.

178 ✦ *Learn Your Pattern of Errors*

We all make mistakes, but we do not all make the *same* mistakes. One person may misspell words often, another may write run-on sentences, another may have trouble choosing the correct verb, and so on. Know the kinds of mistakes you make so you can make a special effort to locate those errors.

Once you know the kinds of mistakes you make, you may also determine under what circumstances you make them. For example, once you discover that you have trouble choosing verbs, a little study of your writing may tell you that you have this trouble whenever you begin a sentence with *there is* or *there are*. This is valuable information because it tells you to check the verbs in any sentences that begin with these words.

179 ✦ *Use an Editing Checklist*

An editing checklist can ensure that you are attending to everything. Use the one below, or devise your own checklist of errors you habitually make. The references in parentheses refer to helpful chapters in the book.

1. Have you read your work aloud to listen for problems? (Chapter 17)

2. Did you check every possible misspelling in a dictionary or with a spell-checker? (Chapter 27)

3. Did you edit for run-on sentences and comma splices? (Chapter 19)

4. Did you edit for sentence fragments? (Chapter 18)

5. Did you check your use of verbs? (Chapter 21)

6. Did you check your use of pronouns? (Chapter 20)

7. Did you check your use of modifiers? (Chapter 22)

8. Have you checked any punctuation you are unsure of? (Chapters 23 and 25)

9. Have you checked your use of capital letters? (Chapter 26)

180 ← *Trust Your Instincts*

Maybe you have had this experience: You have a feeling that something is wrong. However, you cannot give the problem a name, and you are not sure how to solve it. So you skip it and hope for the best. Then you submit your writing, and sure enough—your reader was troubled by the same thing you were troubled by. If you have had this experience, you learned that your instincts are reliable. Because much of what you know about language has been internalized, an inner alarm may sound when you have made a mistake. Always heed that alarm, even if you are not sure what the problem is or how to solve it. Get help if necessary for diagnosing and eliminating the error.

181 ← *Edit More than Once*

Many writers edit once for anything they can find and a separate time for each of the kinds of errors they tend to make.

182 ← *When in Doubt, Check It Out*

When you are unsure about something, look it up in a grammar handbook. If you do not own one, check one out from your library or purchase one.

183 ← *Learn the Rules*

You cannot edit confidently if you do not know the rules. Many people think the grammar and usage rules are understood only by English teachers, but the truth is that anyone can learn them. Invest in a grammar handbook, and each time you make an error, learn the appropriate rule.

184 ← *Get Help*

Ask someone to go over your writing to find mistakes that you overlooked. Be sure, however, that the person who helps you edit is someone who knows grammar and usage rules; otherwise, you will not get reliable information.

185 ← *Use a Computer to Help You Find Your Mistakes*
The following techniques may help you edit with your computer.

Put Your Editing Checklist into a Window. Split your screen, and place your editing checklist (either the one in this chapter or one you devise) into a window. Consult the checklist as you edit.

Quadruple-Space Your Text. Reformat your text with four spaces between each line. This way, you can edit one line at a time with less text entering your visual field to distract you from the words you are studying.

Edit the Screen and the Paper Copy. Edit twice. The first time through, edit on the screen, making the necessary changes as you go. Then print your text and edit a second time on the paper copy. Enter these changes into your file, and print a fresh copy.

Use the Computer's Search Function to Locate Trouble Spots. For example, if you habitually misuse semicolons and confuse *to* and *too*, find every semicolon, *to*, and *too* in your draft and check your usage.

Use the Computer's Grammar Checker—Cautiously. It is not always correct, so evaluate its flags and suggestions, and carefully edit on your own.

Use the Internet. You can find many guides to grammar and usage online. Here are some good ones:

- ccc.commnet.edu/grammar

- snap.com

- powa.org/edit (This website discusses the editing process and has links to pages on grammar and usage.)

18

"I used a period and a capital letter, so why isn't this a sentence?"

You can put a saddle on a donkey, but that won't make it a horse. Similarly, you can start a word group with a capital letter and end it with a period, question mark, or exclamation point, but that won't necessarily make it a sentence.

Troubleshooting Strategies

186 ← *Understand What a Sentence Fragment Is*
If you punctuate a word group as if it *were* a sentence when it cannot be one, you have written a **sentence fragment**.

Word group that cannot be a sentence:	then fell asleep
Sentence fragment:	The child rolled over. Then fell asleep.
Correction:	The child rolled over. Then he fell asleep.

Word group that cannot be a sentence:	Although the election was close
Sentence fragment:	<u>Although the election was close.</u> The losing candidate did not ask for a recount.
Correction:	Although the election was close, the losing candidate did not ask for a recount.

Word group that cannot be a sentence:	such as loyalty, creativity, and integrity
Sentence fragment:	Maria has many admirable traits. <u>Such as loyalty, creativity, and integrity.</u>
Correction:	Maria has many admirable traits, such as loyalty, creativity, and integrity.

187 ← *Isolate Everything You Are Calling a Sentence*

If your draft is relatively short, start at the beginning and place one finger of your left hand under the capital letter. Then place a finger of your right hand under the period, question mark, or exclamation point. Now read the word group between your fingers. If it sounds as if something is missing or if the word group cannot stand alone as a sentence, you probably have a sentence fragment.

Move through your entire draft this way, isolating word groups with your fingers and reading them. Each time you hear a fragment, stop and make the necessary correction. Some people have more success if they read the word groups out loud.

188 ← *Read Your Draft Backward*

Read your last sentence; pause for a moment to consider whether the word group can be a sentence. Then read the next-to-the-last sentence, again pausing to consider. Proceed this way until you have worked back to the first sentence.

189 ← *Check* -ing *and* -ed *Verb Forms*

Sometimes sentence fragments result when *-ing* or *-ed* verb forms stand by themselves. Here are two examples with the *-ing* and *-ed* verb forms underlined:

Fragment: The kitten <u>stretching</u> after her nap.
Fragment: The child <u>frustrated</u> by the complicated toy.

To correct fragments that result when *-ing* or *-ed* verbs stand alone, pick an appropriate verb from this list and add it to the *-ing* or *-ed* form:

is	was	have	had
are	were	has	

Fragment: The kittens <u>stretching</u> after their naps.
Sentence: The kittens <u>are stretching</u> after their naps.
Sentence: The kittens <u>were stretching</u> after their naps.

Fragment: The child <u>frustrated</u> by the complicated toy.
Sentence: The child <u>is frustrated</u> by the complicated toy.
Sentence: The child <u>was frustrated</u> by the complicated toy.

To find fragments that result when *-ing* or *-ed* verbs stand alone, go through your draft checking each *-ing* and *-ed* verb form. Read the sentence with the form, and ask if a verb from the preceding list is necessary. Sometimes, as in the following example, an *-ed* verb *can* stand alone:

Sentence: The kittens <u>stretched</u> after their naps.

190 ← *Check for Fragment-Warning Words*

The following words often begin sentence fragments:

after	as long as	before
although	as soon as	especially
as	as though	even though
as if	because	for example

if	such as	whenever
in order to	unless	where
since	until	wherever
so that	when	while

Check every word group that begins with one of the preceding words or phrases, and make sure the sentence is complete.

However, do not assume that any word group that begins with one of these fragment-warning words is automatically a sentence fragment, because sentences, too, can begin with these words and phrases. To be sure, read aloud to hear whether the words can stand alone as a sentence.

Sentence: While Rudy cleaned the house, Sue cooked dinner.
Fragment: While Rudy cleaned the house.

191 ← *Watch Out for* Who, Whom, Whose, Which, *and* Where

If you begin a word group with *who*, *whom*, *whose*, *which*, or *where* without asking a question, you most likely have written a sentence fragment:

Sentence: Who lives next door?
Fragment: Who lives next door.

Sentence: Whose advice have I valued over the years?
Fragment: Whose advice I have valued over the years.

Look at any word group that begins with *who*, *whom*, *whose*, *which*, or *where*, and make sure that word group is asking a question. If it is not, join the word group to the sentence before it, as illustrated here:

Sentence and fragment: Stavros is a good friend. <u>Whose advice I have valued over the years.</u>
Sentence: Stavros is a good friend, whose advice I have valued over the years.

192 ← *Eliminate the Fragments*

The previous techniques will help you locate sentence fragments; the next two techniques will help you eliminate fragments once you find them. Keep in mind that no one technique will work for every fragment, so if one correction method does not work, try the other.

Join the fragment to a sentence before or after it:

Sentence and fragment: The custom of hat-tipping goes back to the knights. <u>Who would remove their helmets before a lord.</u>

Fragment joined to sentence: The custom of hat-tipping goes back to the knights, who would remove their helmets before a lord.

Fragment and sentence: <u>While trying on the cashmere sweater.</u> Molly snagged the sleeve with her class ring.

Fragment joined to sentence: While trying on the cashmere sweater, Molly snagged the sleeve with her class ring.

193 ← *Add the Missing Word or Words*

To eliminate a fragment that results when a subject, or all or part of the verb, is left out, add the missing word or words:

Sentence and fragment: The auto mechanic assured us the repairs would be minor. <u>Then proceeded to list a dozen things wrong with the car.</u>

Fragment eliminated with addition of the missing subject *he*: The auto mechanic assured us the repairs would be minor. <u>Then he proceeded to list a dozen things wrong with the car.</u>

Fragment:	The surgeon general announcing new nutritional guidelines.
Fragment eliminated with addition of the missing part of the verb *is*:	The surgeon general is announcing new nutritional guidelines.
Sentence and fragment:	Police chiefs want to hire more officers. <u>However, not without additional</u> <u>funds.</u>
Fragment eliminated with addition of the missing subject and verb:	Police chiefs want to hire more officers. However, they cannot do so without additional funds.

194 ✦ *Use a Computer to Help You Check for Fragments*

You can use your computer to find and eliminate sentence fragments.

Reformat Your Paper. To reformat your paper into a list of sentences, press the enter key before each capital letter that marks the start of a sentence. With each word group physically separated, finding fragments can be easier. When you are done with this aspect of editing, reformat your text to draw everything back together.

Use the Grammar Checker—Cautiously. If your word-processing program has a grammar checker, it will flag sentence fragments. Although these programs do a good job of finding fragments, they are not infallible, so double-check each flagged word group, and look for fragments the program might have missed.

Use the Internet. The Guide to Grammar and Writing website has information on fragments, and it links to exercises you can complete for practice. For more information, visit the page on fragments at ccc.comm net.edu/grammar/fragments.htm.

For information on common causes of sentence fragments, visit St. Cloud State University's website at http://leo.stcloudstate.edu/punct/frag mentcauses.html.

19

"How can this be a run-on or a comma splice? It's not even long."

If you have a tendency to write run-on sentences or comma splices, you are not alone. They are two of the most frequently occurring writing errors. Try the following strategies to resolve such errors.

Troubleshooting Strategies

195 ← *Understand What Run-On Sentences and Comma Splices Are*

A **run-on sentence** occurs when two word groups that can be sentences (**independent clauses**) stand together without any separation. A **comma splice** occurs when two word groups that can be sentences (independent clauses) stand together with only a comma between them. Run-on sentences and comma splices are a problem because they blur the points where sentences begin and end.

> **Independent clause:** Charleston Harbor is a fascinating place to visit
> **Independent clause:** many historical attractions are there

A run-on sentence is created when these independent clauses are not separated:

Run-on sentence: Charleston Harbor is a fascinating place to visit
many historical attractions are there.

A comma splice is created when the two independent clauses are separated by nothing more than a comma:

Comma splice: Charleston Harbor is a fascinating place to visit,
many historical attractions are there.

196 ← *Understand How to Separate Independent Clauses*
You can separate independent clauses in three ways:

1. With a comma and coordinating conjunction (*and, but, or, nor, for, so, yet*):

   Charleston Harbor is a fascinating place to visit, <u>for</u> many historical attractions are there.

2. With a semicolon (;):

   Charleston Harbor is a fascinating place to visit<u>;</u> many historical attractions are there.

3. With a period and a capital letter:

   Charleston Harbor is a fascinating place to visit. <u>M</u>any historical attractions are there.

197 ← *Study Sentences Individually*
If your draft is not long, study each of your sentences separately. Place one finger of your left hand under the capital letter and one finger of your right hand under the punctuation end mark. Then identify the number of inde-

pendent clauses (word groups that can stand as sentences) between your fingers. If you have one, the sentence is fine. If you have two or more, be sure you separate the independent clauses as explained in the previous section.

198 ← *Underline Warning Words*
Pay special attention to these words because they often begin independent clauses (word groups that can be sentences):

as a result	furthermore	moreover	similarly
consequently	hence	nevertheless	then
finally	however	next	therefore
for example	in addition	on the contrary	thus

Read over your draft and underline any of these warning words. Then check what is on *both* sides of each underlined word. If—and only if—an independent clause is on *both* sides, place a semicolon (not a comma) before the warning word.

199 ← *Use a Computer to Help You Avoid Run-Ons and Comma Splices*
The strategies that follow will help you locate run-on sentences and comma splices by using computer technology.

Search for Warning Words. Use the search function to find all the run-on warning words (see the preceding strategy). Once these words are identified, check for independent clauses on both sides of these words. Wherever you find independent clauses on *both sides* of a warning word, be sure you have a semicolon before the word.

Isolate Sentences. To reformat your paper into a list, press the enter key before every capital letter marking the beginning of a sentence. This will make it easier to study sentences individually, following the preceding strategies. After finding and eliminating run-ons and comma splices, reformat your text to bring everything back together.

Use the Internet. For information on run-ons and a practice exercise, visit the City University School of New York Law School's website at law.cuny.edu/wc/usage/run_on_sentences.html.

20

"It is I; it is me. What's the difference?"

There you are writing along, and then it happens—you have to use a pronoun and you are not sure which one is correct: Did the police officer issue the warning to Lee and me or to Lee and I? "Lee and me—no, it's Lee and I—no, wait, Lee and me." Ah, what the heck—you pick one and hope for the best. If you stumble over pronouns, the procedures in this chapter can help.

Troubleshooting Strategies

200 ← *Cross Out Everything in the Phrase but the Pronoun*

When a pronoun is joined with a noun, you may be unsure which pronoun to use. Is it "Luis and I" or "Luis and me"? Is it "the girls and us" or "the girls and we"? To decide, cross out everything in the phrase but the pronoun and read what is left:

~~My brothers and~~ I saw the movie six times.
~~My brothers and~~ me saw the movie six times.

With everything but the pronoun crossed out, you can tell more easily that the correct choice is *I*:

My brothers and I saw the movie six times.

Here is another example:

> Dr. Cohen lent ~~Maria and~~ I a copy of the book.
> Dr. Cohen lent ~~Maria and~~ me a copy of the book.

With everything but the pronoun crossed out, you can tell more easily that the correct choice is *me*:

> Dr. Cohen lent Maria and me a copy of the book.

201 ← *Cross Out Words That Rename*

Sometimes words follow a pronoun and rename it:

We baseball players.	(*Baseball players* follows the pronoun and renames it.)
Us sophomores.	(*Sophomores* follows the pronoun and renames it.)
You sports fans.	(*Sports fans* follows the pronoun and renames it.)

To choose the correct pronoun, cross out the words that rename:

> We ~~spectators~~ jumped to our feet and cheered when the band took the field.
> Us ~~spectators~~ jumped to our feet and cheered when the band took the field.

With the renaming word crossed out, the correct choice is clear:

> We spectators jumped to our feet and cheered when the band took the field.

Here is another example:

> Loud rock music can be irritating to we ~~older folks~~.
> Loud rock music can be irritating to us ~~older folks~~.

With the renaming word crossed out, the correct choice is clear:

> Loud rock music can be irritating to us older folks.

202 ← *Add the Missing Words in Comparisons*

Which is it: "Bev is a better foul shooter than I" or "Bev is a better foul shooter than me"? To find out, add the unstated word:

> Bev is a better foul shooter than I am.
> Bev is a better foul shooter than me am.

With the missing word added, you can tell that the correct pronoun is *I*:

> Bev is a better foul shooter than I.

Here is another example:

> John Grisham's new novel interested Miguel as much as I.
> John Grisham's new novel interested Miguel as much as me.

To decide on the correct pronoun, add the missing words:

> John Grisham's new novel interested Miguel as much as it interested I.
> John Grisham's new novel interested Miguel as much as it interested me.

With the missing comparison words added, you can tell that the correct pronoun is *me*.

203 ← *Use* They, Their, *and* Them *with Plural Nouns*

They, their, and *them* refer to plural nouns:

All students should bring their notebooks to the next class; if they forget them, class participation will be difficult.

A problem occurs when *they, their,* or *them* is used to refer to a singular noun:

A person who cares about the environment will recycle. They will also avoid using Styrofoam and plastic.

In the previous sentence, the plural *they* refers to the singular *person*, creating a problem called **lack of agreement**. To eliminate the problem, make the pronoun and noun agree in one of these two ways:

Singular noun and singular pronoun:	A person who cares about the environment will recycle. He or she will also avoid using Styrofoam and plastic.
Plural noun and plural pronoun:	People who care about the environment will recycle. They will also avoid using Styrofoam and plastic.

To ensure agreement, check *they, their,* and *them* to be sure each of these pronouns refers to a plural noun. If it does not, make the noun plural or change the pronoun to a singular form.

204 ← *Remember That* -body, -one, *and* -thing *Words Are Singular*

In formal usage, *anybody, everybody, nobody, somebody, anyone, everyone, no one, someone, anything, everything, nothing, something* (the **indefinite pronouns**) are singular. Therefore, the words that refer to them should also be singular.

Everybody should remember (his or her) admission forms when reporting to orientation.

Someone left (his or her) coat in the auditorium.

Anybody who wants to bring (his or her) family may do so.

Be sure to put everything in (its) place.

Look for the indefinite pronouns. If you find one, look to see if a pronoun refers to it. If so, be sure that the pronoun is singular. Do not rely on the sound of the sentence, because the plural pronoun may sound fine since it is often used in informal spoken English.

205 ← *Circle* Who *and* Whom, *and Underline the Rest of the Clause*

To choose the correct pronoun, circle *who* or *whom* and underline the rest of the **clause** (a word group with a subject and verb). If the circled word acts as a subject, use *who*. If it is the object, use *whom*. Here are some examples:

Hippocrates, (who or whom)? lived around 400 B.C., is called the "Father of Medicine."

Choose *who* because it is the subject of the verb *lived*.

Hippocrates, who lived around 400 B.C., is called the "Father of Medicine."
I attended the lecture by the Holocaust survivor (who or whom)? the community invited to speak.

Choose *whom* because it is the object of the verb *invited*.

I attended the lecture by the Holocaust survivor whom the community invited to speak.

206 ← *Determine the Referent for* You

You addresses the reader. If it refers to someone other than the reader, the result is a problem called **person shift**. To avoid this problem, mentally draw an arrow from *you* to the word it refers to. If this word names someone other than the reader, replace it with the correct pronoun:

Distance runners must train religiously. (You) cannot compete successfully if (you) run only on weekends.

Now here is the corrected version:

Distance runners must train religiously. (They) cannot compete successfully if (they) run only on weekends.

207 ← *Check* It *and* They

Check every *it* and *they* to be sure you have supplied a noun for each of these words to refer to. Otherwise, you will have a problem called **unstated reference**:

Unstated reference:	Charlie is a very curious child. Because of <u>it</u>, he asks questions all the time.
Explanation:	*It* cannot refer to *curious*, because *curious* is a modifier, not a noun. The reference is meant to be *curiosity*, but that word is not stated.
Correction:	Charlie is a very curious child. Because of his curiosity, he asks questions all the time.

Unstated reference:	When I went to the unemployment office, <u>they</u> told me that some construction jobs were available.
Explanation:	There is no stated noun for *they* to refer to.
Correction:	When I went to the unemployment office, the employment counselor told me that some construction jobs were available.

208 ✦ *Avoid Unclear Reference*

When a pronoun can refer to more than one noun, the reader cannot tell what the writer means, creating a problem called **unclear reference**.

Unclear reference:	Dad was in the garage with Brian when he heard the telephone ring.
Explanation:	Because of unclear reference, the reader cannot tell whether Dad or Brian heard the phone.
Correction:	Dad was in the garage with Brian when Brian heard the telephone ring.

209 ✦ *Be Careful of* This *and* Which

To avoid confusion, make sure that *this* and *which* refer to specific nouns:

Confusing:	When people send e-mail, they expect an immediate response, whereas when they send a letter, they do not expect a quick reply. <u>This</u> interests communications specialists. (What interests communication specialists: people expecting an immediate response, people not expecting a quick reply, or the difference in expectations?)
Better:	When people send e-mail, they expect an immediate response, whereas when they send a letter, they do not expect a quick reply. <u>This difference</u> interests communications specialists.

210 ← *Use a Computer to Help You Check Pronoun Usage*

Your word-processing program can help you edit for correct pronoun usage.

Use the Search or Find Function. The search or find function can help you edit efficiently:

• Find and check *they, their, them.* Be sure that these pronouns refer to plural nouns. Also be sure that *they* refers to a stated noun.

• Find and check *anybody, everybody, nobody, somebody, anyone, everyone, no one, someone, anything, everything, nothing, something.* If a pronoun refers to one of these words, be sure it is singular.

• Find and check *who* and *whom.* Subjects should be *who,* and objects should be *whom.*

• Find and check *you.* If it does not refer to the reader, change the pronoun.

• Find and check *which* and *that.* Be sure each refers to a stated noun.

Use the Internet. This University of Colorado at Colorado Springs writing center website provides links to information on many aspects of correct pronoun usage: uccs.edu/~wrtgcntr/handouts/pronouns.html.

This University of North Carolina Web page uses a question-and-answer format to give helpful information on pronouns, and it provides an exercise for practice: http://www2.ncsu.edu/ncsu/grammar/Pronoun3.html.

21

"How do I know which verb form to use?"

Choosing the right verb can be tricky at times, but most of the problems arise in just a few special instances. Strategies for dealing with these instances are discussed in this chapter.

Troubleshooting Strategies

211 ← *Cross Out Phrases Before the Verb*

A phrase before the verb can trick you into choosing the wrong verb form. For example, which is correct?

> The stack of books is about to fall.
> The stack of books are about to fall.

To decide, cross out the phrase *of books*, and you can tell that the correct verb is *is*:

> The stack ~~of books~~ is about to fall.

Phrases before the verb often begin with one of the following words (called **prepositions**):

above	before	inside	over
about	between	into	through
across	by	like	to
after	during	near	toward
among	for	next	under
around	from	of	up
at	in	on	with

When in doubt about the correct verb form, cross out phrases beginning with one of these words. Here are some examples:

The container of old dishes (is or are?) on the landing.
The container of old dishes (is or are?) on the landing.
The container of old dishes is on the landing.

The herd of steers (graze or grazes?) contentedly.
The herd of steers (graze or grazes?) contentedly.
The herd of steers grazes contentedly.

The characteristics of the German shepherd (make or makes?) him a
   suitable show dog.
The characteristics of the German shepherd (make or makes?) him a
   suitable show dog.
The characteristics of the German shepherd make him a suitable show
   dog.

212 ← Rewrite Questions

In sentences that ask questions, the verb comes before the subject. Verb choice is easier if you rewrite the sentence so it is no longer a question:

Sentence with question:	(<u>Have</u> or <u>has</u>?) the students finished taking exams?
Sentence rewritten:	The students <u>have</u> finished taking exams.
Sentence with question and correct verb:	<u>Have</u> the students finished taking exams?

213 ← *Rewrite Sentences Beginning with* Here *and* There

When a sentence begins with *here* or *there*, the verb comes before the subject. When uncertain, rewrite the sentence putting the subject before the verb. The correct choice should be easier that way:

Sentence with *here*:	Here (<u>is</u> or <u>are</u>?) the important papers you asked for.
Sentence rewritten:	The important papers you asked for <u>are</u> here.
Sentence with *here* and correct verb:	Here <u>are</u> the important papers you asked for.
Sentence with *there*:	There (<u>was</u> or <u>were</u>?) an excellent dance band playing at the wedding reception.
Sentence rewritten:	An excellent dance band <u>was</u> playing at the wedding reception.
Sentence with *there* and correct verb:	There <u>was</u> an excellent dance band playing at the wedding reception.

214 ← *Watch Out for Subjects Joined by* Or *and* Either/Or

Whether subjects joined by *or* and *either/or* (called **compound subjects**) take a singular or plural verb depends on what subjects are joined.

1. If both subjects are singular, use a singular verb:

   (Joyce) or (Rico) expects to pick me up for the concert.

   Either the (steak) or the (veal roast) is on sale at the market.

2. If both subjects are plural, use a plural verb:

   The (boxes) or the (fishing poles) are behind the door.

   Either the (scouts) or their (leaders) visit the elderly every week.

3. If one subject is singular and the other is plural, place the plural subject second and use a plural verb:

   The (gardenia) or the (roses) make a lovely centerpiece.

   Either my (sister) or my (brothers) cook Thanksgiving dinner each
   year.

215 ← *Watch Out for Indefinite Pronouns*

The **indefinite pronouns** are *each, either, neither, one, none, no one, nothing, nobody, anyone, anybody, anything, everyone, everybody, everything, someone, somebody,* and *something.*

   In formal usage, these indefinite pronouns take singular verbs—even though the sense of the sentence suggests that a plural verb is logical. When you have used one of these words as the subject of a sentence, mentally circle the word and draw an arrow to the verb. Then check that verb to be sure it is singular.

(Each) of the students wants (not want) to have the test on Friday so the
weekend is more relaxing.

(One) of the first museums was (not were) the Altes Museum in Berlin.

(Either) of these vacation plans <u>meets</u> (not <u>meet</u>) your needs.

(Neither) of these paintings <u>suits</u> (not <u>suit</u>) my taste.

(None) of Lin's excuses <u>is</u> (not <u>are</u>) believable.

Do not rely on the sound of the sentence, because the plural verb may sound fine and the singular verb may sound a little off. This is because the plural verb is often used in informal speech and writing. Nonetheless, use the singular verb for strict grammatical correctness in formal usage.

216 ← *Understand Verb Tenses*

Tense means "time." Different verb tenses indicate different times.

1. Use the **present tense** to show the following:

   Something is happening now: The committee members <u>are meeting</u> in room 2.

   Something happens regularly: Each year, the summer hurricane season <u>worries</u> coastal residents.

   Something is true indefinitely: She applied to Ohio State University, which <u>is</u> in Columbus, Ohio.

2. Use the **past tense** to show that something took place before now:

   The television series <u>was cancelled</u> after two episodes.
   Cass <u>left</u> for the store before I <u>arrived</u>.

3. Use the **future tense** to show that something has not happened yet, but will.

   Next fall, the downtown reconstruction <u>will begin</u>.

4. Use the **present perfect tense** to show the following:

Something began in the past and continues into the present:	Already you <u>have painted</u> half of the kitchen.
Something began in the past and recently ended:	Jake <u>has</u> finally <u>finished</u> the test.
Something happened at an unspecified time in the past:	I <u>have visited</u> Spain twice.

5. Use the **past perfect tense** to show that something happened in the past before something else happened in the past:

Dimitri said that Sophia <u>had left</u> before I arrived.

6. Use the **future perfect tense** to indicate one future event will occur before another future event:

By the end of the year, I <u>will have completed</u> a psychology minor.

If you are unsure how to form the various verb tenses, consult a grammar handbook.

217 ← *Listen to Your Verb Tenses*

Many verbs change their form to show different tenses (times):

Present tense (time):	Today I <u>walk</u> two miles for exercise.
Past tense (time):	Yesterday I <u>walked</u> two miles for exercise.
Future tense (time):	Tomorrow I <u>will walk</u> two miles for exercise.

Sometimes a change in verb tense is necessary to show a change in time, but if you change the tense inappropriately, you create a problem called **tense shift:**

Appropriate change in tense from present to past:	I <u>recall</u> that April Fools' Day <u>began</u> in France.
Problematic tense shift from present to past:	After I <u>finish</u> my work, I <u>watched</u> a movie.

Read your draft out loud and listen to your verb tenses. If there are problem tense shifts, you are likely to hear them.

218 ✦ *Use a Computer to Help You Solve Verb Problems*

If you compose at the computer, you can try the following strategies to edit for verb problems.

Use the Search or Find Function. Use the search or find function to locate the indefinite pronouns provided earlier in this chapter. If you discover some used as subjects, make sure the verb form is correct.

Use the Grammar Checker—Cautiously. If your word-processing program includes a grammar checker, it will flag many verb-form problems. Because grammar checkers are not always reliable, study each flagged verb yourself. Also, look for errors the computer does not flag.

Use the Internet. For information on using the correct verb and for practice exercises, visit ccc.commnet.edu/grammar/sv_agr.htm.

For information on verb tense shifts, visit the Massachusetts Institute of Technology website at http://web.mit.edu/writing/Writing_Process /verbtenseshifts.html.

"I'm unsure about modifiers."

A **modifier** is a word or phrase that describes. Consider this sentence:

Because of the terrible accident, traffic moved slowly.

Because *terrible* describes *accident, terrible* is a modifier; because *slowly* describes *moved, slowly* is a modifier. Modifiers take different forms in different grammatical settings.

Troubleshooting Strategies

219 ✦ *Know When to Use an Adjective and When to Use an Adverb*

Which sentence is correct?

The party ended so <u>abruptly</u> that no one had a chance to eat.
The party ended so <u>abrupt</u> that no one had a chance to eat.

If you are unsure, you may have trouble knowing when to use adjectives and when to use adverbs. An **adjective** describes a noun or pronoun, and an **adverb** describes a verb or other modifier. Frequently, the adverb form ends in *-ly* and the adjective form does not:

Adjectives	Adverbs
brief	briefly
swift	swiftly

loud	loudly
clear	clearly

When in doubt, mentally draw an arrow from the modifier to the word it describes. If the arrow goes to a noun or pronoun, use the adjective form. If the arrow goes to a verb or modifier, use the adverb form. Here is an example.

> Diane mowed the lawn (quick or quickly?) so she could leave with her friends.

To decide, mentally draw an arrow from the modifier to the word described. If the word described is a noun or a pronoun, use the adjective; if it is a verb or another modifier, use the adverb (which often ends in *-ly*):

> Diane mowed the lawn (quick or quickly?) so she could leave with her friends.

Now you can tell that *quickly* is called for because a verb is described:

> Diane mowed the lawn quickly so she could leave with her friends.

Here are some more examples:

> David was (absolute or absolutely?) sure of the answer.

> David was absolutely sure of the answer. (A modifier is described, so the adverb is used.)

> The ancient Egyptians thought of the soul as a bird that could fly around (easy or easily?).

> The ancient Egyptians thought of the soul as a bird that could fly around easily. (A verb is described, so the adverb is used.)

Chris is ((happy or happily?)) that he was promoted after only one
month on the job.

Chris is happy that he was promoted after only one month on the job.
(A noun is described, so the adjective is used.)

220 ← Remember That Good *Is an Adjective and* Well *Is an Adverb—with One Caution and One Exception*

Good is an adjective; it describes nouns and pronouns:

The good news is that I got the job.

Well is an adverb; it describes verbs and modifiers:

After ten years of lessons, Maxine plays the piano well.

Now here's the caution: after verbs like *taste*, *seem*, *appear*, and *look*, use
good because the noun or pronoun before the verb is being described.

The meat tastes good, even though it is overcooked.

Claudia looks good, although she just had surgery.

Now here's the exception: *Well* is used as an adjective to mean "in good
health."

After six brownies and a bottle of soda, the child did not feel well.

221 ← *Do Not Use* More *or* Most *with an* -er *or* -est *Form*

Yes: I like tacos better than nachos.

No: I like tacos more better than nachos.

Yes: The Sahara Desert is the world's <u>hottest</u> region in summer.

No: The Sahara Desert is the world's <u>most hottest</u> region in summer.

Yes: The Sahara Desert is <u>bigger</u> than the United States.

No: The Sahara Desert is <u>more bigger</u> than the United States.

Yes: The <u>rainiest</u> place on earth is Mount Waialeale, in Hawaii.

No: The <u>most rainiest</u> place on earth is Mount Waialeale, in Hawaii.

222 ← *Check Sentences That Open with* -ing *or* -ed *Verb Forms*

An *-ing* or *-ed* verb form (called a **participle**) can be used as an adjective:

Whistling, Carolyn strolled through the park.

Whistling is a verb form that is used as an adjective to describe *Carolyn*.

Living only two or three years, lizards have a short life span.

Living is a verb form used as an adjective to describe *lizards*.

When an *-ing* or *-ed* form opens a sentence, it must be followed by the word that the form describes. Otherwise, the result will be a **dangling modifier**. Dangling modifiers can create silly sentences:

Dangling modifier: While making the coffee, the toast burned.
(This sentence says that the toast made the coffee.)

Correction: While making the coffee, I burned the toast.
(The opening *-ing* verb form is followed by a word it can sensibly describe.)

Dangling modifier:	Exhausted from work, a nap was needed. (This sentence says that the nap was exhausted.)
Correction:	Exhausted from work, Lucy needed a nap. (The opening *-ed* verb form is followed by a word it can sensibly describe.)

If you are in the habit of writing dangling modifiers, check every opening *-ing* and *-ed* verb form to be sure it is closely followed by a word it can sensibly describe.

223 ✦ *Move Modifiers Near the Words They Describe*

If a modifier is too far from the word it describes, the result is a **misplaced modifier**. A misplaced modifier can create a silly sentence:

Misplaced modifier:	Lee bought a bicycle from a neighbor with a flat tire. (The sentence says that the neighbor had a flat tire.)
Correction:	Lee bought a bicycle with a flat tire from a neighbor. (The modifier has been moved closer to the word it describes.)

224 ✦ *Use a Computer to Help with Modifiers*

If you compose at the computer, you can try the following strategies.

Use the Search or Find Function. Use the search or find function to find and check each use of *good* and *well*.

Use the Grammar Checker—Cautiously. If your word-processing program includes a grammar checker, it will flag many errors with modifiers. However, grammar checkers are not always reliable, so check each flagged error yourself, and look for errors the computer did not flag.

Use the Internet. These sites provide information on modifiers:
- bartleby.com/64/1.html
- edufind.com/english/grammar/get_alpha.cfm?letter=A

23

"Can't I just place a comma wherever I pause?"

Placing commas wherever you pause is an unreliable method of punctuating: sometimes it works and sometimes it doesn't. Your best bet is to learn the rules. Editing strategies are given in this chapter to help you follow these common comma rules:

- Use a comma after an introductory element.
- Use a comma before a coordinating conjunction that joins independent clauses.
- Use a comma to separate items in a series.
- Use a comma to set off nonessential sentence elements.

For other important comma rules, consult a grammar handbook.

Troubleshooting Strategies

225 ← *Find the Subject, and Look in Front of It*

Most of the time, anything that comes before the subject of a sentence is an **introductory element** and should be set off with a comma. It does not matter whether the material is one word, a phrase, or a clause. Thus, once you identify the subject of a sentence, you can look in front of it. If there are any words there, follow them with a comma, like this:

subject

Word before the subject: Surprisingly, the <u>heart of a whale</u> beats
only nine times a minute.

subject

Phrase before the subject: In medieval Japan, <u>fashionable women</u>
blackened their teeth to enhance their
appearance.

Clause before the subject: Although Albert Einstein developed the

subject

theory of relativity, <u>he</u> failed his first college entrance exam.

226 ↫ *Find the Coordinating Conjunctions, and Then Look Left and Right*

The following words are **coordinating conjunctions**; you can remember
them by remembering *fanboys*, the word formed by the first letter of each
word.

for	or
and	yet
nor	so
but	

If a coordinating conjunction joins two word groups that each can stand as
a sentence (**independent clause**), place a comma before the conjunction.

To apply this rule, mentally circle every coordinating conjunction; then
look left and right. If an independent clause appears on both sides, place
a comma before the conjunction.

independent

independent clause   clause

Use comma: [I enjoy reading Stephen King novels], (but) [I do not
enjoy watching horror movies.]

independent clause   independent clause

Use comma: [The Centers for Disease Control predicts a flu outbreak], (so) [I plan to get a flu shot.]

independent clause   independent clause

Use comma: [Fish can distinguish colors], (and) [they actually prefer some colors over others.]

not a clause

Do not use comma: The owl cannot move its eyes (but) [can turn its head around.]

not a clause

Do not use comma: The car accelerated quickly (and) [turned left.]

not a clause

Do not use comma: You can leave with me now (or) [wait until later.]

227 ← *Look for Series*

A **series** is three or more words, phrases, or clauses. Separate the items in a series with commas.

Words in a series: This restaurant specializes in <u>pasta</u>, <u>steak</u>, <u>salads</u>, and <u>seafood</u>.

Phrases in a series: Recycling centers have been established <u>at the government center</u>, <u>behind the high school</u>, and <u>at the baseball fields</u>.

Clauses in a series: <u>The manager lowered prices</u>, <u>the sales staff tried to be more helpful</u>, and <u>the owner remodeled the store</u>.

228 ← *Identify Nonessential Elements*

A **nonessential element** can be removed without changing the meaning of the sentence. Identify nonessential elements and set them off with commas. In the following sentences, the nonessential elements are underscored as a study aid.

Nonessential word: The president at the time, Carter, worked to achieve the Egyptian-Israeli peace agreement.

Nonessential word: The governor, surprisingly, opposed the balanced-budget amendment.

Nonessential phrase: You can, of course, join us for dinner.

Nonessential phrase: The crime rate, according to the newspaper, has not increased this year.

Nonessential clause: Very few people understand how the election process works, if you ask me.

Nonessential clause: Karen Carpenter, who died of anorexia nervosa, was a talented performer.

229 ← *Use a Computer to Help You Check Comma Usage*

If you compose at the computer, try the following strategies to edit for commas.

Use the Delete Key. If you are unsure whether an element is nonessential and, therefore, should be set off with commas, delete the element and see if necessary meaning is lost. If necessary meaning is *not* lost, use commas. After deciding, put the deleted element back in the sentence. For example, in the following sentence, is the underlined element nonessential?

Sgt. Shepherd who was awarded a Purple Heart is reenlisting.

Use the delete key to get

Sgt. Shepherd is reenlisting.

Because necessary meaning is not lost without the element (we can still tell who is reenlisting), the element is nonessential. Therefore, use commas:

Sgt. Shepherd, who was awarded a Purple Heart, is reenlisting.

Here is another sentence. Is the underlined element nonessential?

The sergeant <u>who was awarded a Purple Heart</u> is reenlisting.

Use the delete key to get

The sergeant is reenlisting.

Necessary meaning is lost because without the element, we cannot tell which sergeant is reenlisting. Therefore, the element is essential and commas are not used:

The sergeant who was awarded a Purple Heart is reenlisting.

Use Underlining. If you are unsure whether to use a comma before a coordinating conjunction, underline the words before and after the conjunction. Examine both sets of words. If *each* set can stand as a sentence, use the comma. If neither set can be a sentence or if only one can be a sentence, do *not* use a comma.

Use the Internet. Visit this page from the Capital Community College Guide to Grammar and Writing website for an explanation of comma rules and practice exercises: ccc.commnet.edu/grammar/commas.htm.

24

"What if I want to quote somebody?"

Sometimes, you want to use words that someone has spoken or written: those words may advance a story, add vividness, lend insight into character, or provide support for an idea. When you quote someone, you are obligated to get it right. That means you must reproduce the words *exactly* as they were spoken or written, and it means you must follow the punctuation and capitalization rules in this chapter.

Troubleshooting Strategies

230 ↩ *Consider Where in the Sentence the Quotation Occurs*

If your quotation comes *after* the statement of who spoke, model this form:

Eli reminded us, "Remember to put out the campfire before retiring."

If your quotation comes *before* the statement of who spoke, model this form:

"Remember to put out the campfire before retiring," Eli reminded us.

If your quotation comes both before and after the statement of who spoke, model the first form if the first part does *not* form a sentence. Model the second form if it does.

> "Remember," Eli reminded us, "to put out the campfire before retiring."
> "Remember to put out the campfire before retiring," Eli reminded us. "You don't want to start a forest fire."

231 ✦ *Determine Whether the Quotation or the Entire Sentence Asks a Question*

When the quotation asks a question, model one of these forms:

> The reporter asked Senator McEwin, "Did you vote for the trade bill?"
> "Did you vote for the trade bill?" the reporter asked Senator McEwin.

When the entire sentence asks a question, model this form:

> Did the newspaper say, "The president of the school board plans to resign"? (The question mark appears outside the quotation mark.)

232 ✦ *Reproduce a Person's Thought as a Quotation*

A person's thoughts are treated like spoken words:

> Julia thought, "It's time I made a change in my life."

233 ✦ *Be Sure You Really Have Exact Words*

Before using quotation marks, be sure you are reproducing someone's exact words:

Use quotation marks (exact words):	The police officer said, "Move your car."
Do not use quotation marks (not exact words):	The police officer said that you should move your car.

234 ← *Use the Computer to Check Your Use of Quotations*

If you compose at the computer, consider the following strategies.

Use the Grammar Checker—Cautiously. If your word-processing program includes a grammar checker, it will flag many misused quotation marks. However, grammar checkers are not always reliable, so check each flagged error yourself, and look for errors the program did not flag.

Use the Internet. A convenience of using the Internet is the ability to copy and paste material from websites. However, *any* material you copy must appear in quotation marks and must be acknowledged.

25

"I have trouble with apostrophes."

A postrophes have two main functions: they take the place of missing letters in contractions, and they signal possession. Some people think apostrophes have a third function: to drive them crazy. Apostrophes *can* be pesky, so if you are unsure how to use them, try the techniques in this chapter.

Troubleshooting Strategies

235 ← *Identify the Missing Letter(s) in a Contraction*

A **contraction** is formed by taking two words, dropping one or more letters, and joining the two words into one. In contractions, place the apostrophe at the site of the missing letter(s). For example, the contraction form of *did not* is *didn't*. Because the *o* is left out of *not*, the apostrophe is placed between the *n* and the *t*.

Here are some more examples:

have + not = haven't (apostrophe at site of missing *o*)
we + will = we'll (apostrophe at site of missing *wi*)
it + is = it's (apostrophe at site of missing *i*)

Note: The contraction form of *will not* is the unusual *won't*.

236 ← Use It's *Only When You Can Substitute* It Is *or* It Has

1. *It's* is the contraction form of *it is* or *it has*.

   It's time for a change of leadership in this state. (It is time for a
   change of leadership in this state.)
   It's been ten years since I smoked a cigarette. (It has been ten years
   since I smoked a cigarette.)

2. *Its* is a possessive form; it shows ownership and cannot be substituted
   for *it is* or *it has*.

   Yes: The river overflowed its banks. (*Its* shows ownership.)
   No: The river overflowed it's banks.

   Yes: It's too late to turn back now. (*It's* here means *it is*.)
   No: Its too late to turn back now.

237 ← *Avoid Contractions*
No law says that you *must* use contractions. If you are unsure where to
place the apostrophe, use the two-word form instead of the contraction.

238 ← *Use the of Test*
If you can add a phrase beginning with *of* to a noun or indefinite pronoun
and reword, the noun or indefinite pronoun is possessive and needs an
apostrophe to indicate possession:

Is an apostrophe needed?	The books pages are beginning to curl.
Add an *of* phrase:	The pages of the book are beginning to curl.
Apostrophe is needed:	The book's pages are beginning to curl.

Is an apostrophe needed?   <u>Someones car</u> is parked in a no parking zone.

Add an *of* phrase: The <u>car of someone</u> is parked in a no parking zone.

Apostrophe is needed: <u>Someone's car</u> is parked in a no parking zone.

Is an apostrophe needed?   The <u>steak knives</u> on the counter are very sharp.

Add an *of* phrase: The <u>knives of steak</u> on the counter are very sharp.

No apostrophe is needed: The <u>steak knives</u> on the counter are very sharp.

239 ← *For Possessive Forms, Ask Two Questions*

Apostrophes are used with nouns to show possession. To determine how to use the apostrophe, ask, "Does the noun end in *s*?"

1. If the noun *does not* end in *s*, add an apostrophe and an *s*, like this:

   President + 's = President's
   The President's Council on Aging reports an increase in
      homelessness among the elderly.
   children + 's = children's
   Children's toys cost more money than they are worth.

2. If the noun *does* end in *s*, ask, "Is the noun singular or plural?"

   a. If the noun is singular, add an apostrophe and an *s*, like this:
      Delores + 's = Delores's
      Delores's new car was hit in the parking lot.
      bus + 's = bus's
      The bus's brakes jammed, causing a minor accident.

b. If the noun is plural, add an apostrophe, like this:
shoes + ' = shoes'
All the shoes' laces are too long.
mayors + ' = mayors'
The three mayors' mutual aid agreement will yield economic benefits.

240 ← *Watch Out for Possessive Pronouns*

These words are **possessive pronouns** because they show ownership: *his, hers, yours, theirs, ours,* and *its.* Since these words are already possessive, do not use them with apostrophes. (Remember that *its* is the possessive pronoun, and *it's* is the contraction form of *it is* and *it has.*)

Yes: His backpack was left in the car.
No: His' backpack was left in the car.

Yes: Are the sneakers under the couch yours?
No: Are the sneakers under the couch your's?

241 ← *Use a Computer to Help You Check Apostrophe Usage*

If you compose at the computer, you may like the following strategies.

Use the Spell-Checker—Cautiously. Many programs do not check apostrophes in contractions, so misspellings such as *cant* will not be noted. Also, your spell-checker will not distinguish between *its* and *it's.*

Use the Internet. To test how well you use apostrophes, visit this Web page: primaryresources.co.uk/online/apostrophes.htm.

26

"I never know what to capitalize."

Ask people how they know what to capitalize, and many will say they aren't sure, so they just capitalize "the important stuff." Are you one of those people? If so, how do you know what's "important"? This chapter can help you use capital letters with more confidence.

Troubleshooting Strategies

242 ↩ *Capitalize the Names of Animals, People's Names, and the Titles Before People's Names*

Capitalize:	John, Lassie, Seabiscuit, Aunt Rhoda, Professor DeMatteo, Rabbi Gold
Do not capitalize:	boy, dog, horse, my aunt, a professor, the rabbi

Note: Always capitalize the pronoun *I.*

243 ⬳ *Capitalize Titles of Relatives Substituted for Names*

Capitalize: I bought <u>Mother and Dad</u> a DVD player for their anniversary.

Do not capitalize: I bought <u>my mother and dad</u> a DVD player for their anniversary.

244 ⬳ *Capitalize Specific Geographic Locations, Names of Nationalities, and Adjectives Derived from Them*

Capitalize: Africa, Grand Canyon, Baltic Sea, Atlanta, Georgia, Mahoning Avenue, Stark County, Route 82, the Middle East, the Pacific Northwest, the West Coast, Chinese cooking, Irish linen

Do not capitalize: continent, a canyon, sea, city, one state, the avenue, county, the northwestern region, the western part of the country

245 ⬳ *Capitalize Religions, Sacred Books, and Words and Pronouns That Refer to God*

Capitalize: God, the Lord, Allah, the Torah, the New Testament, Muslim, Catholicism, the Holy Bible, the Trinity, Jewish, In His wisdom, God is just.

Do not capitalize: the gods, a deity, a sacred text

246 ⬳ *Capitalize Specific Days, Months, and Holidays*

Capitalize: Monday, June, Halloween
Do not capitalize: day, month, holiday, winter

247 ← *Capitalize Specific Name Brands*

Capitalize: Mountain Dew, Pillsbury cake mix, Reebok tennis shoes, Cheerios, Buick

Do not capitalize: soda pop, cake mix, tennis shoes, cereal, car

248 ← *Capitalize Specific Organizations, Companies, and Buildings*

Capitalize: General Motors, Disney World, Indiana University, the Empire State Building, the Fraternal Order of Police, the Red Cross

Do not capitalize: car manufacturer, amusement park, college, building, fraternity, club, company

249 ← *Capitalize Specific Historic Events, Documents, and Periods*

Capitalize: the Constitution of the United States, the Battle of the Bulge, Korean War, the Magna Carta, the Renaissance

Do not capitalize: a country's constitution, a battle, the war, document, historical period

250 ← *Capitalize Titles Correctly*

Capitalize the first and last word of a title and a subtitle, no matter what those words are. In between, capitalize everything except articles (*a, an, the*), short conjunctions (*and, but, or, nor, for, so, yet, since*), and short prepositions (*in, on, at, of, by*).

In the Heat of the Night
Star Wars: The Wrath of Khan

The Catcher in the Rye
Making Peace with Your Past: How to Be Happy

251 ← *Use a Computer to Check Capitalization*

If you compose at the computer, the following strategies can help you capitalize correctly.

Use the AutoCorrect Feature. Your word-processing program may allow you to correct automatically words you routinely capitalize incorrectly. For example, in Microsoft Word use AutoCorrect by clicking on "Tools" in the menu bar and then on "AutoCorrect." In the "Replace" box, type the word as you do when you capitalize it incorrectly (e.g., *civil war*). In the "With" box, type the word with correct capitalization (*Civil War*).

Use the Spell-Checker—Cautiously. Your computer's spell-checker is more likely to find errors in words you have not capitalized than in words you have capitalized inappropriately.

Capitalize in E-Mail Correctly. In e-mail you write for school, work, or other formal and semiformal occasions, follow the capitalization rules. Using all capital letters is like electronic shouting; using all lowercase letters can be confusing.

Use the Internet. For rules for capitalization, visit this Web page: ccc.commnet.edu/grammar/capitals.htm.

27

"I can't spell."

First the bad news: misspelled words are a problem because they lead the reader to question your ability. Now the good news: many capable people do not spell well, but they have learned ways to solve their spelling problem. You, too, can eliminate misspellings with the techniques in this chapter.

Troubleshooting Strategies

252 ✦ *When in Doubt, Check It Out*
When it comes to using a dictionary, we all get lazy. Still, the only surefire way to check a spelling is to look up the word. If you have the slightest suspicion that a word is misspelled, check the dictionary.

253 ✦ *Buy Two Dictionaries*
To make looking words up as convenient as possible, buy two dictionaries: a hardback collegiate dictionary to keep on your writing desk and a fat paperback to carry with you to other locations where you write—such as work. You are more likely to look up a word if you have a dictionary at hand and do not have to get up and walk somewhere to get one.

254 ✦ *Use a Pronunciation Dictionary*
If you have trouble finding words in a traditional dictionary, try using a pronunciation dictionary that lets you find words according to the way they sound.

255 ← *Use a Spelling Dictionary*

Spelling dictionaries, available in most drugstores and bookstores, reference frequently misspelled words. They provide spellings without definitions, so they are thin and convenient to carry around.

256 ← *Use a Pocket Spell-Checker*

Pocket spell-checkers are electronic gadgets about the size of some calculators. They can be expensive, but if you are more inclined to check spellings with an electronic gizmo than with a dictionary, they are worth the money.

257 ← *Learn Correct Pronunciations*

Sometimes people misspell because they pronounce a word incorrectly. For example, you may misspell *February* if you pronounce it "Feb-u-ary"; you may misspell *preventive* if you pronounce it "pre-ven-ta-tive."

258 ← *Break a Word into Parts*

When a word is composed of identifiable parts, spell the word out part by part so it is more manageable:

under-stand-able	dis-ease
with-hold	comfort-able
arm-chair	lone-liness
room-mate	over-coat
kinder-garten	

259 ← *Break a Word into Syllables*

Some words are more easily spelled if you go syllable by syllable. Words of three or more syllables are often better handled this way:

or-gan-i-za-tion	hos-pi-tal
cit-i-zen	in-di-vis-i-ble

mon-u-men-tal
Jan-u-ar-y
in-vi-ta-tion

con-ver-sa-tion
pro-ba-bly

260 ← *Look for Prefixes*

When a **prefix** (word beginning) is added to a word, the spelling of the base word will usually not change:

mis-take
dis-satisfaction
mis-spell
un-nerve
un-necessary

pre-pare
mis-inform
inter-related
pre-record

261 ← *Use Memory Tricks*

Think of tricks to help you spell words. For example, the word *instrument* contains *strum*, and you strum a guitar, which is an instrument. Actors in a *tragedy* often *rage* at each other.

Memory tricks can be particularly helpful for pairs of words that are often mistaken for each other. You may find some of the following tricks to your liking, and you may want to make up tricks for other pairs of words that you confuse.

1. advice/advise

   • *Advice* means "a suggestion."

   Joel's <u>advice</u> proved sound.

   • *Advise* means "to give advice."

   Yvette is the best person to <u>advise</u> you.

   Memory trick: A person with a <u>vice</u> needs ad<u>vice</u>.

2. affect/effect

- *Affect* means "to influence."

  The drought will <u>affect</u> the economy for years to come.

- *Effect* means "result."

  The <u>effects</u> of the drought are devastating.

Memory trick: The first syllable of *effect* rhymes with the first syllable of result.

3. among/between

- *Among* is used for more than two.

  Divide the candy <u>among</u> the four children.

- *Between* is used for two.

  The difference <u>between</u> the ages of Phil and Carlos is not important.

Memory trick: Can you fit anything <u>between</u> the two *e*'s in the last syllable of *between*?

4. beside/besides

- *Beside* means "alongside of."

  I parked the van <u>beside</u> the Corvette.

- *Besides* means "in addition to."

  <u>Besides</u> good soil, the plants need water.

Memory trick: The final *s* in *besides* is "in addition to" the first *s*.

5. fewer/less

- *Fewer* is for things that can be counted.

  <u>Fewer</u> people voted in this election than in the last one.

- *Less* is used for things that cannot be counted.

  People who exercise regularly experience <u>less</u> stress than those who do not.

Memory trick: Think of *countless. Less* is used for things that cannot be counted.

6. then/than

- *Then* refers to a certain time.

  The trumpets blared; <u>then</u> the cymbals crashed.

- *Than* is used to compare.

  I like small classes better <u>than</u> large lectures.

Memory trick: Think of the *e* in *then* and *time*; think of the *a* in *than* and *compare.*

262 ← *Learn the Homophones*
Homophones sound alike, but they are spelled and used differently. Learn the following homophones and any others that give you trouble:

1. all ready/already

- *All ready* means "all set."

  By three o'clock, the family was <u>all ready</u> to leave for Virginia Beach.

- *Already* means "by this time."

  We are <u>already</u> an hour behind schedule, and we haven't begun the trip yet.

2. its/it's

- *Its* shows ownership.

  The car hit a pothole and broke <u>its</u> axle.

- *It's* is the contraction form of *it is* or *it has*.

  It's too late to say you are sorry.

  It's been ten years since graduation.

3. passed/past

   - *Passed* means "went by" or "handed."

   Katie passed the potatoes to Earvin.

   The shooting star passed overhead at nine o'clock.

   - *Past* refers to previous time. It also means "by."

   I have learned from past experience not to trust Jerry.

   When I drove past the house, no one was home.

4. principal/principle

   - *Principal* means "main" or "most important." It is also the school official.

   The principal roadblock to peace is the personalities of the country's leaders.

   The high school principal favors a dress code.

   - *Principle* is a truth or standard.

   The principles of world economics are studied in this course.

5. there/their/they're

   - *There* refers to direction or place. It also opens sentences.

   Place the vase of flowers there on the coffee table.

   There is a surprise for you in the kitchen.

   - *Their* shows ownership.

   The students revised their drafts in the computer lab.

- *They're* is the contraction form of *they are.*

  Do not sit Lee and Dana next to each other; they're not getting along.

6. threw/through

   - *Threw* is the past tense of *throw.*

     The shortstop threw the ball to the pitcher.

   - *Through* means "in one side and out the other" or "finished."

     I had trouble getting the thread through the needle.

     My morning biology class is not through until eleven o'clock.

7. to/too/two

   - *To* means "toward." It is also used with a verb to form the **infinitive**.

     Liza usually walks to school.

     Eric is learning how to play the violin.

   - *Too* means "excessively" or "also."

     I find it too hot in this building.

     Juanita works in the library, and she tutors math too.

   - *Two* is the number.

     Two weeks ago, I bought a new car.

8. your/you're

   - *Your* shows ownership.

     You left your keys in the car.

   - *You're* is the contraction form of *you are.*

     If you're leaving now, please take me with you.

263 ↞ *Underline Words to Check Later*

While drafting or revising, you may sense that a word is spelled wrong. Yet looking the word up at that point is undesirable because it interrupts your drafting or revising momentum. To solve this problem, underline every word whose spelling you are unsure of as you write. Then you have a visual reminder to look up the word later, when it is more convenient.

264 ↞ *Keep a Spelling List*

Look up the words you misspell and add these words, correctly spelled, to a list for study. Each day, study the list and memorize another word or two in an effort to increase the number of words you can spell.

265 ↞ *Use a Computer to Help You with Your Spelling*

If you compose at the computer, these tips can help you spell correctly.

Use the AutoCorrect Feature. Your word-processing program may allow you to correct automatically the words you routinely misspell. For example in Microsoft Word, use AutoCorrect by clicking on "Tools" in the menu bar and then on "AutoCorrect." In the "Replace" box, type the word as you do when you misspell it (e.g., *defanite*). In the "With" box, type the word spelled correctly (*definite*).

Use the Spell-Checker—Cautiously. Spell-checkers test every word you have written against the words in the dictionary in the computer's memory. If a word is not recognized, the spell-checker will offer alternative spellings. If the spell-checker comes across a typing error, it may be baffled if nothing in its memory comes close to the spelling. In this case, it will not know what to suggest as a correct spelling. Also, homophones (soundalikes) are untouched by spell-checkers, so the confusion of something like *there*, *their*, and *they're* will not be resolved. Finally, resist the temptation to accept automatically the first spelling offered by a spell-checker, as it may not be the one you should use. Despite these limitations, spell-checkers can be helpful to people with chronic spelling problems.

Use the Internet. The following sites may be helpful:

- To check spellings, you can use the Merriam-Webster online dictionary at m-w.com.
- For spelling rules, visit gsu.edu/~wwwesl/egw/susan.htm.
- For a list of common homonyms, visit http://literacy.kent.edu/Mid west/Materials/ndakota/spelling/lesson1.html.

Index